Carmen Bouldin **Jeff Bouldin**

Jeanie Smith

Copyright © 2025 Carmen Bouldin All rights reserved

This book is a work of fiction. Any references to historical events, real people, or real places are used fictitiously. Other names, characters, places, and events are products of the authors' imaginations, and any resemblance to actual events or places or persons, living or dead, is entirely coincidental.

No part of this book may be reproduced, or stored in a retrieval system, or transmitted in any form or by any means, electronic, mechanical, photocopying, recording, or otherwise, without express written permission of the publisher.

ISBN: 978-1-967407-05-7

Outside and Inside Cover designs: J. A. Smith

Any Edgar Allan Poe tales or poetry quotes used in this book are in the public domain.

DEDICATIONS

To Poe, with Love

I want to thank the Poe Museum and the Edgar Allan Poe Society of Baltimore for the online resources that you so kindly provide for free. Without your wealth of Poe history and facts, this book would not be possible. A thank you goes out to Sydney and Josh Hardison, my stepdaughter and my son-in-law, for all the recipe ideas and titles with puns they contributed. A huge thank you goes out to Holly Knightley for giving us the title of the book, The Flavored Raven. I'd like to thank Jeanie Smith, my Poe Other, for her creativity, artistry, and intelligence in working toward finishing this collection. "The POEcast is strong with this one." Last, but not least, I would like to thank the love of my life, Jeff Bouldin, who helped with innovative ideas and creating recipes. Without his cocksmithing credentials, our cocktails would have been flat.

Love, Carmen Bouldin

I never dreamed a part of my life would have Edgar Allan Poe in it until my wife, Carmen, came into the picture. I always knew, "that's the author who wrote 'The Raven,'" but now I have a better appreciation for him. I dedicate this book to Carmen because we were able to work on this together. Thank you to my amazing daughters Sydney, Lindsey, and Zoe. I am so proud of the women they have become. I also want to thank my two son-in-laws, Josh and Evan, who are like sons to me now. Last, but not least, I can't wait to share in the experiences my first grandchild, Cecilia, will have.

Jeff Bouldin

To my mom, miss and love you

My first memories involve a book. Whether it was the Bible my grandfather would read to me as we sat on the front porch or a sleepy time lullaby my mom read to put my baby mind to rest. Those words on a page did the opposite. They ignited and inspired my imagination, allowing a new world to grow in my mind. It has been many years since those days, but thanks to my POEtastic partner, Carmen Bouldin, I get to continue this with the reintroduction of one of my favorite authors in my life, Edgar Allan Poe. Through the opportunity Carmen gave me to help on the POEcast, we have combined our love of creativity with our knowledge to hopefully bring others into a whole new POE world!

Love, Jeanie

THE POWER OF POE

"How did Edgar Allan Poe enter your life?" A question we always ask our Gothic Guests. We firmly believe we should answer this question related to our POEcast, The Six Degrees of Edgar Allan Poe. Jeanie and I have always loved Poe's tales and poems since elementary school. We are teachers of English and history; thus, Poe has always traveled with us in our teacher bag of tools ready to be unleashed on young minds waiting to be wowed. However, what about wowing adults about Poe? Jeanie said it best on our last Poe Discussions in September of 2025:

And some of them fall in love with the Goth part of "The Raven" and "Annabel Lee." But what they really fall in love with is later, when they find out about Poe's own life and his own tragedies–it led to where he was. And I think if more kids and more people knew about what he had to go through to get even halfway through his life, more people would be tuned in to his work and to how he came up with all those wonderful stories and the horror of it all. And, like you said, it's not about the gore. It's not about, you know, disembodied anything. It's all about the psychological. It's the emotional undercurrent with the macabre. And I mean, he was a genius at it; he did it so well.

So, back in 2021, when I was thinking of doing a podcast about Poe, I researched to find no real podcasts about the man. The only podcasts were other people conducting readings of Poe's works or performing adaptations–there were no Poe discussions at all. I knew Jeanie loved Poe, so I asked her to do the podcast with me. We felt that it needed to be about Poe's influences on other people and their work; however, our content must be general, but honed in specific areas. Thus, the title of our podcast was born: The Six Degrees of Edgar Allan Poe. We took the premise of six degrees of separation, creating six areas we could focus on Poe's influences.

Those degrees became: Literature, Pop Culture, Science/SciFi, Horror, Surrealism, and Poe Places. Within these degrees, we have so many possibilities. "And that's one of the reasons why Jeanie and I started the podcast was because we saw all these influences that Poe had, and they're endless. It's like we could do this podcast forever because we'll never run out of people that have been influenced by Poe." I posited on our latest Poe Discussions September 2025.

With Literature, we get to focus on his satire, poetry, essays, and celebrate him being the father of detective fiction. Pop Culture provides so many opportunities where Poe is adapted into art, in television shows and movies, in cartoons, in plays, in music, in games, and so many more mediums. Poe loved science and wrote his own scientific theories with Eureka, and he is credited with writing some of the first sci/fi short stories. Horror continues to be what Poe is known for, giving us so many ways to focus on the influential legacies he gift wrapped to us, making horror the gift that keeps on giving with new adaptations. Many times, Poe's stories and poems provide a trance into surrealism, considering surrealism was not coined until 1917. Poe lived in many places, leaving historical records of life in the mid-1800s and the effects on those places in modern times.

As Kris Kringle states in the movie *Miracle on 34th Street*, "Oh, Christmas isn't just a day, it's a frame of mind." Edgar Allan Poe is not just a writer, he is a literary genius; moreover, he is a Renaissance man who dabbled in many different worlds within his works, including cryptology, mesmerism, phrenology, cosmology, forensics, death, technical writing, the poetic principle, criticisms, languages, classical studies, mythology, history, and the list goes on...forevermore.

The Power of Poe lives on with all who read his works upon first meeting him in middle school or junior high, or meeting him in college, or hearing about him in conversation, or seeing his collections in book stores. He is limitless and neverending. Many people become fanatical about Poe just like Jeanie and me. "The Poe cult is not confined to any one, two or three countries. It has spread throughout the civilised world. It includes the cultured people of Europe, America, and in the lands beyond the sea. It has made Edgar A. Poe a classic." Concluded Eugene L. Didier from The Poe Cult. The Poe community is one of amity and acceptance; we welcome all into the Poe world to celebrate one of the greatest writers of all time. This compilation is not just a recipe book; it is a dedication to the bestowal of the oeuvre Mr. Poe bequeathed to all of us upon being...Nevermore.

The Six Degrees of Edgar Allan "Tiki" Poe

1.5oz Cognac
1.5oz Amontillado
1oz Blood Orange juice
.5oz Falernum
.25oz Simple Syrup (2 to 1 mix)
4 dash Smoked Chili Bitters

Our signature cocktail, The Six Degrees of Edgar Allan "Tiki" Poe, contains six ingredients to represent our six degrees:

> Literature = Cognac
> Pop Culture = Smoked Chili Bitters
> Science/Sci-Fi = Simple Syrup
> Horror = Blood Orange Juice
> Surrealism = Falernum
> Poe Places = Amontillado

Combine all ingredients into a shaker and shake over ice. Strain into a glass and fill with pebble ice. Enjoy and wait for a Raven to visit. Listen for the sound of a beating heart. Think of all the lost loves in your life.

TABLE OF CONTENTS

1	LITERATURE	*1-26*
2	POP CULTURE	*27-44*
3	SCIENCE FICTION	*45-60*
4	HORROR	*61-78*
5	SURREALISM	*79-98*
6	POE PLACES	*99-136*
7	THE MASQUE OF THE RED DEATH FEAST	*137-152*
	THE FALL OF THE FLAVORED RAVEN	*153-154*

APPENDIX	*155-158*
INDEX	*159-164*
RESOURCES	*165-168*
ABOUT THE AUTHORS	*169-176*

LITERATURE 6°

CHAPTER

ONE

ANNABEL LEE

> "For the moon never beams without bringing me dreams"
>
> *"Annabel Lee" - 1849*

INGREDIENTS

2 oz. Melon Liqueur

1 oz. Moonshine

1 ½ oz. Lemon Juice

1 ½ oz. Lime Juice

½ oz. Rich Simple Syrup

⅛ tsp. Sea Salt

INSTRUCTIONS

Add ice to a tin, add all ingredients, top off and shake until the tin is very cold. Add one large round ice cube to a rocks glass. Strain the drink into the glass. By shaking the ingredients in the tin, it will create a small amount of foam, mimicking the night-tide of the sounding sea.

See Appendix for more information on Rich Simple Syrup

History

Sour cocktails are some of the earliest drinks on record. The first mention of a sour cocktail is from 1856, and the first written documentation is from 1862. Sour cocktails predominantly include spirits, water, sugar, and citrus. Many sour cocktail recipes, especially those of the whiskey variety, include an egg white to the mixture to add frothiness. An egg white can be added to the *Annabel Lee* cocktail. For this variation, do not add ice to the tin. Add all ingredients for the recipe, including the egg white. Shake the tin until blended-this is referred to as dry shaking-so the egg white develops a large amount of foam. Add ice to the tin, shake again until the tin is cold, and strain into a rocks glass over one large circular ice cube. The foam creates a smooth, silkiness added to the cocktail, creating more of the tides rolling in from the sea.

Inspiration

The poem, "Annabel Lee," is one of our favorite poems, telling the story of a love who passed and the immense grief the speaker feels. The ingredients for the cocktail represent elements from the poem. For example, the green shade of the melon liqueur represents "the winged seraphs in Heaven coveted her and me" and "the angels, not half so happy in Heaven, envying her and me." The moonshine was added to represent "for the moon never beams without bringing me dreams." The tart mixture of the lemon and lime juice provides the feeling of bitterness, "So that her high-born kinsmen came and bore her away from me." The simple syrup shows the beauty of their love, "And this maiden she lived with no other thought than to love and to be loved by me." Lastly, the sea salt represents specifically the poem's setting, "It was many and many a year ago, in a kingdom by the sea."

POE'S POETRY

> "Helen, like thy human eye
> There th' uneasy violets lie"
>
> *"The Valley of Unrest" - 1831*

INGREDIENTS

1 oz. Moonshine

1 oz. Floral Gin*

½ oz. Creme de Violette

¼ oz. Elderberry Liquor*

⅛ tsp. Sea Salt

INSTRUCTIONS

Add all ingredients into a mixing glass or cocktail tin over ice. Stir until the mixing glass is chilled on the outside. Double strain into a martini glass and serve.

*For the Gin, we suggest Hendricks Gin and for the Elderberry Liquor, we suggest St. Germain.

Inspiration

For Poe's Poetry, we wanted to bring a cocktail to you filled with all of Poe's poetic brilliance all mixed up into one. We took many elements from several of his poems, such as "The Valley of Unrest" (1831), "To One in Paradise" (1843), "Dream-Land" (1844), and "Eulalie" (1845). We focused on the natural landscape Poe included in many poems with the moon, flowers, and the sea added to the color violet, which was utilized in several poems. We hope you enjoy this poetic, floral cocktail as you read one of Poe's nature poems sitting by a lake in springtime.

MIDNIGHT DREARY

> "Once upon a midnight dreary"
>
> *"The Raven" - 1845*

INGREDIENTS

1 oz. Mr. Black

1 oz. Cognac

1/2 oz. Blanco Mezcal

2 dashes Smoked Chili Bitters

INSTRUCTIONS

Put ingredients in a mixing glass, stir over ice until chilled. Double strain into a coupe glass.

Inspiration

"The Raven" is by far Poe's most iconic poem, written in trochaic octameter. To honor this gothically crafted musical verse, we devised a cocktail pulling out the elements of fire. The poem sets up the narrator on a grim evening where he would most likely have been sitting by the fireside. The smoky elements mixed with coffee and cognac notes, which could be spicy, floral, or woody depending on the type of cognac, will have you closing your eyes dreaming of a stately raven sitting on the bust of Pallas above your chamber door, keeping you warm upon a midnight dreary evening.

TARPAULIN'S TODDY

> "Bobbing up and down, for a few seconds, like an apple in a bowl of toddy, he [Tarpaulin], at length, finally disappeared amid the whirlpool of foam which, in the already effervescent liquor, his struggles easily succeeded in creating."
>
> *King Pest - 1835*

INGREDIENTS

3/4 cup water

2 oz. Tennesssee Whiskey

1 Spoonful of Honey

1/2 oz. Lemon Juice

2 oz. Apple Cider, non-alcoholic

INSTRUCTIONS

Place the boiled water into a mug. Add the lemon and honey until the honey is dissolved. Add the apple cider and whiskey; stir until blended. Garnish with a cinnamon stick.

History

Being from Tennessee, we had to choose the short story, *King Pest*, for one of our recipes. The namesake of the story, King Pest, was based on the president at the time, Andrew Jackson. His presidential term occurred from 1829-1837. Poe wrote *King Pest* as political satire with undercurrents of critique for Jackson's programs.

Inspiration

Just as the quote for this cocktail states, Tarpaulin was bobbing like an apple in a toddy, which gave us the inspiration for this cocktail. Arch Duchess Ana-Pest was insulted by Tarpaulin to the point where she threw him in a bowl of ale and the quote provides a comparison of what Tarpaulin looked like after he was thrown. With the connection to Tennessee, a Tennessee whiskey was the key ingredient for this hot toddy. Make this cocktail on a cold winter's night and read *King Pest* for the dark humor.

FOUR BEASTS IN ONE

> "Heavens! the town is swarming with wild beasts!"
>
> *Four Beasts in One - 1833*

INGREDIENTS

1 pkg Cocktail Sausages

3 oz. pkg Prosciutto Ham

1 pkg Thin Salami Slices

1 pkg Pepperoni Slices

2 cans Crescent Rolls

INSTRUCTIONS

Preheat oven to 375 degrees. Divide each crescent roll into thirds. Wrap a partial slice of ham, salami, and pepperoni around the cocktail sausage. Wrap the crescent roll around the four meats. Place on a flat baking pan, making several of these up. Bake in the oven for around 12-15 minutes or until golden brown.

*pkg - package

Inspiration

Poe's tale, *Four Beasts in One,* is full of satire and entertainment. The one beast with four parts can be supposed to be made up of a camel, lion, man, and panther. Our recipe does not call for these specific four ingredients, fortunately; however, we decided to take a common appetizer recipe most people know and enhance it with vigor. Pigs in a Blanket, as we know, contains little sausages wrapped in some type of crescent roll and baked. Adding three more types of protein to the mix, creates a flavor enhanced meat in a roll appetizer worthy of calling it *Four Beasts in One,* adding the emphasis on the word beasts.

TARR AND FETHER'S CHICKEN BACON CORN CHOWDER

> "— and thus to refuse him any other diet for a week than that which properly appertains to a chicken. In this manner a little corn and gravel were made to perform wonders."
>
> *The System of Dr. Tarr and Professor Fether* - 1845

INGREDIENTS

1.5 lb. small red potatoes, cut into 1-inch cubes

1/2 onion, chopped

2 bags (12 oz each) frozen whole kernel corn

1 32-oz carton or 4 cups chicken broth

1 tsp salt

1 tsp ground white pepper

1 Tbsp Bell Pepper Herb or 1 diced bell pepper

1 tsp Oregano

1/2 tsp ground mustard

1 tsp Old Bay

1 Tbsp minced garlic

2 cups half-and-half

2 Tbsp cornstarch

1 lb. bacon, crisply cooked, crumbled

2 chicken breasts

*lb.- pound, *Tbsp - tablespoon, *tsp - teaspoon

INSTRUCTIONS

In slow cooker, layer onions, chicken, spices, potatoes, corn, and broth. Cover; cook on Low heat setting 6-7 hours or until potatoes are tender. After you have started the crockpot, at some point while this is cooking, cook the bacon according to directions on the package. We cook the bacon in the oven around 400 degrees for ten minutes, take out and flip the bacon to the other side, and then cook ten minutes more.

After cooking for 6 hours, in a small bowl, beat half-and-half and cornstarch with whisk until smooth. Stir half-and-half mixture and cooked/crumbled bacon into mixture in slow-cooker. Cover; cook 1 hour longer or until slightly thickened.

Inspiration

The System of Doctor Tarr and Professor Fether is another one of Poe's satires, albeit very dark. In the short story, an unnamed narrator visits an asylum where the "doctors" are providing soothing treatments for the patients. When we decided on the recipe to pay homage to this story, we thought of the old saying, "tar and feather," meaning public humiliation after adding hot tar and chicken feathers for punishment. The title hints at this phrase. In reading this, the quote we chose mentions a diet of chickens, and then later mentions corn. We felt this recipe was a satirical way to showcase Poe's dark tale.

THE BURGERS IN THE RUE MORGUE SOUP

> "You shall give me all the information in your power about that affair of the murder in the Rue Morgue."
>
> *The Murders in the Rue Morgue -*
> 1841

INGREDIENTS

*2 lb.s. Ground beef
3 Tbsp Garlic, minced
3/4 Onion, chopped
2 tbsp Montreal steak seasoning
1 tsp Salt
1 tsp Pepper

**4 cups Beef broth
3 Russet Potatoes peeled and cubed
2 14.5 oz cans of diced tomatoes

***Cheddar Cheese Sauce
1 1/2 cup whole milk
2 Tbsp butter
2 Tbsp All Purpose Flour
2 Cup Shredded Cheddar Cheese
1/4 tsp Salt

*lb.- pound, *Tbsp - tablespoon, *tsp - teaspoon

INSTRUCTIONS

*Cook all ingredients together in a skillet and transfer to a soup pot.

**Put broth, potatoes, and tomatoes in soup pot with beef mixture. Bring to a boil and reduce to low temperature. Cook for 20 minutes.

***Melt butter in a sauce pan over medium heat. Whisk in flour and salt until paste forms. Slowly add milk, cook and stir until fully incorporated - about 2 minutes. Add cheese. Cook and stir until the cheese is melted - about 2 minutes.
Once potatoes are cooked through add 1/2 cup Yellow Mustard and cheese sauce. Stir in until blended, cook 5 minutes on low.
Chop up Dill pickles slices and put on top of soup after putting it into a bowl. If desired, use a bread bowl.

Inspiration

Cheeseburgers have nothing to do with the first detective story ever created; however, adding a pun to the title, *The Murders in the Rue Morgue*, by Poe, makes for a fun recipe to create. All three of us love murder mysteries and puns, so thanks to Jeff's daughter and son-in-law, Sydney and Josh, the name, The Burgers in the Rue Morgue was born. We thought how cool would it be to create a cheeseburger soup with potatoes. It takes on a new way of burgers and fries for dinner. So, if you are craving burgers and fries, try this recipe for an innovative approach to an American classic dinner.

DIDDLING CUCUMBER SALAD

> "He is cool—cool as a cucumber. He is calm—calm as a smile from Lady Bury. He is easy — easy as an old glove, or the damsels of ancient Baiæ."
>
> *Diddling as Considered One of the Exact Sciences - 1843*

INGREDIENTS

4-5 mini cucumbers, sliced
1 ½ cup cherry tomatoes, halved
¾ cup sweet peppers, cored and diced
¼ Cup Olive oil*
14 Cup Balsamic Vinegar*
Salt
Pepper
Garlic Powder
Other Seasoning**

INSTRUCTIONS

Wash and prepare ingredient vegetables in a mixing bowl. Add salt, pepper, and garlic powder to taste. **Add other seasoning - this can be any type of seasoning you want to use. If you want more of an Italian salad, add Italian seasoning. If you want it to be more of a Cajun salad, add a little cayenne pepper and paprika, etc. You can also just add some type of seasoning mix. *For the olive oil and vinegar, we also use flavored styles. If you find a store that carries flavored oils and vinegars, it is fun to pair them to create these dressings for this salad.

History & Inspiration

This recipe was adapted by Jeff from the southern style tomato, onion, and cucumber salad with Italian dressing. He only likes cooked onions, so he thought, "Why not add sweet peppers instead?" His recipe is one we eat, especially in the summer, when the vegetables can be purchased at local farmer's markets. We have fun using the different oils and vinegars to switch things up.

As for Poe's short story about diddling, you will have to read it and find out what he means by diddling. Get ready for another one of his satirical comedies and laugh out loud. We were inspired to use this salad recipe due to the simile, "as cool as a cucumber," Poe used. Especially in the summer, this salad will keep you "cool" from the heat.

POLITIAN BUTTERNUT SQUASH

> "Of butternuts, gingerbread, and milk and water!"
>
> *Politian – 1835*

INGREDIENTS

1 butternut squash, peeled and cut in chunks
1 Tbsp Olive oil
2 Tbsp butter, melted
1 tsp brown sugar
1/4 tsp minced garlic
1/4 tsp minced ginger
1/8 tsp salt
1/8 tsp pepper

INSTRUCTIONS

Preheat the oven to 400 degrees. Place cut squash in a bowl and add spices and wet ingredients. Mix up, making sure spices cover squash. Spray a baking sheet with an oil spray, and place mixture on it. Bake in the oven for 23 minutes.

*Tbsp - tablespoon, *tsp - teaspoon

History & Inspiration

Politian is Poe's unfinished and only play. The setting of the play is in 16th century Rome, containing a murder, where Poe adds in envy and revenge. The play is actually based on the true story of the murder of Solomon P. Sharp that occurred in 1825. The story is fascinating, odd, and a must read.

Just as we did for many other recipes, we chose a food mentioned in the story. Butternut squash is quite delicious, seemingly similar to sweet potatoes or yams, but not as stringy. Carmen created this recipe, thinking garlic and ginger would be savory spices for this side dish, mixed with a little brown sugar. If you like sweet and savory together, you are in for a treat.

THE PEPPER "BELLS"

"To the tintinnabulation that so musically wells
From the bells, bells, bells, bells"

The Bells - 1849

INGREDIENTS

1 lb. Ground Beef
½ lb. Ground Pork Sausage
2 Eggs
1 Tbsp Onion, diced
½ tsp. Sage
¾ tsp. Salt
¼ tsp. Pepper
2 Cans Tomato Soup
1 Cup Cooked Rice
10 Bell Peppers, Halved and Deseeded

INSTRUCTIONS

Preheat the oven to 350 degrees. Cook rice as you are preparing bell peppers and other ingredients. Combine one can of tomato soup with equal parts water to the soup can (add water to the soup can after placing the soup in a small mixing bowl), and set this bowl aside.

Continued on next page...

*lb.- pound, *Tbsp - tablespoon, *tsp - teaspoon

Directions Cont.

Combine ground beef, ground pork sausage, eggs, onion, sage, salt, pepper, and 1 can of tomato soup. Once rice is fully cooked with no water remaining, add the rice to the mixture. Spoon meat mixture into each bell pepper halve and place in a 9x13 baking dish or roasting pan. Depending on the size of the peppers, you may need to additionally use an 8x8 or 9x9 baking dish if you run out of room. Once all peppers are stuffed, pour the mixture of the second can of tomato soup and water mixture over the peppers where the juice lays nicely on each pepper and the juice run-over is on the bottom of the baking dish. Bake for 1 hour at 350 degrees.

Inspiration

Poe wrote the rhythmical poem, "The Bells," in 1848, and it was one of the last poems to be published because he died in October 1849. This poem can be sung because of the beautiful melody that flows within his words. He talks of silver bells, golden bells, brazen bells, and iron bells as if he is musing through the stages from birth to death. There is a chorus throughout the poem woven within the stanzas to bring forth the musical quality so beautiful. We thought this recipe would honor this poem with its delicious taste bringing music to your taste buds with the "tintinnabulation" of the spices added.

THE PUR"LOIN"ED LETTUCE WRAPS

> "Well, then; I have received personal information, from a very high quarter, that a certain document of the last importance, has been purloined from the royal apartments."
>
> *The Purloined Letter* - 1844

INGREDIENTS

3-5 lb. Pork Loin Roast

Crushed Pineapple or Fresh Pineapple (if using fresh, a 16 oz. package is what we used)

Salt & Pepper to taste (we used ½ Tbsp. of each)

1 Tbsp. Garlic Powder

1 6 oz. can Pineapple juice

1 ¼ Cup Water

1-2 Heads of Romaine Lettuce

Teriyaki Sauce or Sundried Tomato Dressing for Optional Dipping

INSTRUCTIONS

Mix together the salt, pepper, and garlic powder. Rub the pork loin with this mixture and then place the pork loin roast in a crockpot. Add pineapple and all the juice from the container. Add one 6 oz. can of pineapple juice. Add 1 ¼ cup water (Make sure you are covering the mixture; we filled the pineapple juice can with water three times and poured in). Cook around 8 hours on low or until the roast is falling apart. Serve roast and pineapple mixture on romaine lettuce by wrapping the lettuce up around the mixture and close with toothpicks. The wraps taste wonderful just like this; however, the teriyaki sauce or sundried tomato dressing can be nice for dipping.

*lb.- pound, *Tbsp - tablespoon, *tsp - teaspoon

Inspiration

The Purloined Letter is Poe's third and last detective fiction story with the renowned detective, C. Auguste Dupin, along with his sidekick, an unnamed narrator. The police prefect comes to Dupin with the issue of a letter being stolen from the Queen, which could damage her reputation. This is a tale of blackmail and mystery; however, Dupin solves the case of the whereabouts of the missing letter with finesse.

The elements of the choice of recipe to celebrate this grand tale does not come from the tale itself, just the name, The Purloined Letter, changing the name using the pun of The Pur "loin"ed Lettuce Wraps as well as changing the Letter to Lettuce. Poe enjoyed humor and satire and we are sure he would have approved of this pun to celebrate his great mystery.

KINGDOM BY THE SEA-SALT CARAMEL BLACK VELVET CUPCAKES

> "It was many and many a year ago,
> In a kingdom by the sea,"
>
> *"Annabel Lee"* - 1849

INGREDIENTS

- 1 Stick of Butter
- 2 ½ Cups All Purpose Flour
- 1 ¼ Cups Sugar
- 1 tsp. Baking Soda
- 1 tsp. Sea Salt
- ¼ Cup Cocoa Powder
- ½ Cup Vegetable Oil
- ⅝ Cup Buttermilk
- 3 Eggs
- 1 tsp. Vinegar
- 1 tsp. Vanilla Extract
- Black Gel Food Coloring
- 1 package of Kraft Caramel Bits

*lb.- pound, *Tbsp - tablespoon, *tsp - teaspoon

INSTRUCTIONS

Preheat oven to 350°. Set butter out for room temperature. In a separate bowl, mix together the dry ingredients: Flour, baking soda, sea salt, and cocoa powder. In another bowl, cream the butter and sugar together first. Add the vanilla extract, vinegar, oil, buttermilk, and eggs.

Slowly add in the dry ingredients. Add food coloring (any food color can be substituted if you like). Add the package of caramel bits and mix with a spoon. Dip the batter into cupcake pan(s) with cupcake liners. Lightly sprinkle a little sea salt to the tops of each cupcake. Bake for 25 minutes. If you grease your pan instead of using liners, bake for 22-25 minutes. Yields 24 cupcakes.

Frosting

2 8 oz. packs of Cream Cheese
1 Stick of Butter
1 tsp. Vanilla Extract
2-3 Cups of Powdered Sugar
Food Coloring

Set cream cheese and butter out for room temperature. Cream together and add the vanilla extract. Slowly mix in the powdered sugar. Add food coloring for the desired color you would like. Frost cupcakes once they are cooled off.

Inspiration

The Kingdom by the Sea-Salt Caramel Black Velvet Cupcakes spring out from one of Poe's most popular poems, "Annabel Lee," published posthumously in 1849. To honor his spectacularly beautiful poem, we decided to create a scrumptious cupcake with elements of the "sea" salt. Additionally, what better type of cake to honor Poe than a velvet cake, but rather than red velvet, we used black velvet. Many artists' renderings of Annabel Lee portray her to be a raven haired beauty. Black velvet represents Annabel Lee's luxurious locks flowing in the wind, unfortunately chilling and killing her. Several ladies claim to be Annabel Lee; however, that is one secret that went to the grave with Poe. No proof has ever been found to reveal who she was in real life. Not knowing the true identity leaves us with a romantically gothic feeling of undying love as we celebrate this love with this decadent dessert.

POP CULTURE 6º

CHAPTER

TWO

QUOTH THE RAVEN, "EAT MY SHORTS!"

> "Quoth the raven, Nevermore."
>
> *"The Raven" - 1845*

INGREDIENTS

1 1/2 oz. Angel's Envy Bourbon

1 oz. Blanco Mezcal

3/4 oz. Blue Curacao

1/2 oz. Amontillado

1/2 oz. Butterscotch Schnapps

1/4 oz. Lemon Juice

INSTRUCTIONS

Add ice to a tin, add all ingredients, top off and shake until the tin is very cold. Add one large round ice cube to a rocks glass. Strain the drink into the glass. By shaking the ingredients in the tin, it will create a small amount of foam, mimicking the night-tide of the sounding sea.

History

The Simpsons television show began a traditional Halloween special each year called The Treehouse of Horror. The first special ran on October 25, 1990, featuring one segment dedicated to Poe's "The Raven." Among Poe fans, this episode resonates as a brilliant nod to including Poe into pop culture.

Inspiration

The ingredients were inspired from elements in the episode. The characters, Lisa and Maggie, play angels; thus, Angel's Envy bourbon was chosen. The amontillado is a nod to Poe's "The Cask of Amontillado" and the butterscotch schnapps is a nod to Bart's love of Butterfinger candy bars.

SQUEAKY BOOTS

> "Villains!" I shrieked, "dissemble no more! I admit the deed!"
>
> The Tell-Tale Heart - 1843

INGREDIENTS

1 1/2 oz. Don Q Puerto Rican Rum

1 oz. Dr. Byrd's Pineapple Rum

1/2 oz. Lime Juice

1 oz. Pineapple Juice

1/2 oz. Rich Simple Syrup

1/4 oz. Bitterman's Tiki Bitters

1/4 oz. Allspice Dram

1/16 Tsp. Sea Salt

INSTRUCTIONS

Add all ingredients into a cocktail mixing tin. Add crushed ice and shake until tin is cold on the outside. Pour into a mai tai glass or a preferred pineapple tiki mug. To with crushed ice. Garnish with a small pineapple chunk, adding cloves for eyes, nose, and mouth to create Spongebob. Add an umbrella for fun.

History

We decided to take the inspiration from this Spongebob episode and create a tiki cocktail since Spongebob lives in a pineapple.

Inspiration

On the Spongebob episode, "Squeaky Boots," which aired on September 17, 1999, Mr. Krabs tricks Spongebob into taking a pair of boots instead of a paycheck. As Spongebob keeps wearing them, the boots continue to squeak and it drives Mr. Krabs' guilty conscience into madness just like the narrator in Poe's *The Tell-Tale Heart*.

THE DARK KNIGHT

> "...I do not hesitate to say that legitimate deductions even from this portion of the testimony — the portion respecting the gruff and shrill voices — are in themselves sufficient to engender a suspicion which should bias, or give direction to all farther progress in the investigation of the mystery."
>
> *Murders in the Rue Morgue - 1841*

INGREDIENTS

2 oz. Royal Jamaican Dark Rum

1/2 oz. Mr. Black

6 Blackberry

1 Bar Soon Rich Demerara Simple Syrup

1 Bar Spoon Fee Brother's Black Walnut Bitters

INSTRUCTIONS

Place 6 blackberries into a mixing glass. Add simple syrup and Bitters. Muddle until blackberries are fully mashed. Add Mr. Black and Rum. Add ice and stir until chilled. Double strain over ice in a rocks glass. Garnish with a blackberry.

Inspiration

In 2003, DC Comics began a series where a 19th century Batman and Edgar Allan Poe team up to find a serial killer. Contained within five volumes, Poe becomes a Dupinlike detective alongside Batman. What better way to pay homage to this crime fighting duo than this dark, sweetly bitter nutty cocktail while reading about Poeman.

THE POE TOASTER

> "Drink," I said, presenting him the wine.
>
> He raised it to his lips with a leer. He paused and nodded to me familiarly, while his bells jingled.
>
> "I drink," he said, "to the buried that repose around us."
>
> "And I to your long life."
>
> *The Cask of Amontillado - 1846*

INGREDIENTS

1 1/2 oz Four Roses Small Batch

1 oz Cognac

2 bar spoons Rich Demerara Simple Syrup

1 bar spoon Fee Brothers Black Walnut Bitters

INSTRUCTIONS

Add ice to the cocktail mixing glass, add all ingredients, and then stir until chilled. Strain into a coop glass.

History

The date of 1949 on the anniversary of Poe's birth is the most accepted year of the Poe Toaster's first appearance. This gentleman began leaving a partially full bottle of cognac and three red roses on Poe's grave. The cognac's significance is unknown, but scholars believed the three roses represent the three people buried under Poe's headstone: Edgar Allan Poe, Virginia Clemm Poe, and Maria Clemm. In 1993, a note was left saying the torch of this tradition would be passed on and in 1999, another note provided information that someone else had been passed the responsibility of this tradition. In 2009, which was the bicentennial of Poe's birth, the visits had stopped.

Inspiration

We wanted to honor The Poe Toaster for adding more mystery to Poe's legacy. A few of the ingredients have meaning for this cocktail. Paying homage to the toaster, we added cognac. We decided on Four Roses Small Batch because The Poe Toaster left three roses; thus, the fourth rose is in honor of him. Mix this cocktail up on Poe's birthday and raise a toast to the Poe Toaster.

THE PRICELESS POE

> "Drink," I said, presenting him the wine.
>
> He raised it to his lips with a leer. He paused and nodded to me familiarly, while his bells jingled.
>
> "I drink," he said, "to the buried that repose around us."
>
> "And I to your long life."
>
> *The Cask of Amontillado - 1846*

INGREDIENTS

2 oz. Spanish Tempranillo Wine

1 oz. Rhum Agricole

¾ oz. Ancho Reyes Chile Liqueur

½ oz. Licor 43

½ Barspoon of Old Forrester Smoked Cinnamon Bitters

INSTRUCTIONS

Pour all ingredients into a mixing glass over ice. Stir until the outside of the glass is cold. Strain into a rocks glass over a large ice cube. Garnish with a cinnamon stick.

History

Roger Corman directed eight Edgar Allan Poe films for American International Pictures with Vincent Price as the lead in seven of those films. The seven Price/Poe films are as follows: *The House of Usher* 1960, *The Pit and the Pendulum* 1961, *Tales of Terror* 1962, *The Raven* 1963, *The Haunted Palace* 1963, *The Masque of the Red Death* 1964, and *The Tomb of Ligeia* 1964. Corman and Price brought a resurgence to Poe's works as they were adapted through Corman's style of giving a back story connected to Poe while Poe's short story would be the third act. Every character Price played, he became with brilliance and fidelity as if he conversed with Poe himself. His Roderick Usher portrayal is the best we have ever seen. What better combination than The Master of the Macabre meshed with the Master of Horror. Vincent Price was and remains one of the greats, leaving us a legacy of films to savor and a humanitarian to admire with his work in the arts and the culinary world.

Inspiration

For what Roger Corman and Vincent Price gave us with the seven Poe films they made together, we wanted to pay homage. We took elements out of each of the films and combined them in a spooky cocktail ready to drink upon watching one of these pictures. You will not be disappointed with this recipe. Mix the drink, sit down in your armchair with a Poe tale, and read it in your mind as Vincent Price narrates it to you.

LONELY HEARTS CLUB PEPPER DIP

> "I started, hourly, from dreams of unutterable fear, to find the hot breath of the thing upon my face"
>
> *The Black Cat - 1843*

INGREDIENTS

8 oz. Cream Cheese, softened
16 oz. Sour Cream
2 Packs of Ranch Seasoning Mix
1 tsp. Onion Powder
1 tsp. Garlic Powder
1 tsp. White Pepper
1/4 tsp. Salt
1 Green Bell Pepper
6 Sweet Peppers
1 Jalapeño

INSTRUCTIONS

With a hand mixer, mix cream cheese and sour cream until smooth. Mix in spices. Deseed all peppers. Use a food processor to finely chop the peppers. Stir in the peppers and your dip is ready to eat.

*oz. - ounce, *tsp. - teaspoon

Inspiration

When you look at the cover of The Beatles' album, *Sgt. Pepper's Lonely Hearts Club Band*, you see Edgar Allan Poe at the very top smack dab in the center in between Carl Jung and Fred Astaire. The Beatles released this album in 1967. All the people included on the cover were those whom the Beatles admired. Poe was also named in their song, "I am the Walrus," which was a song they wrote to create nonsense on purpose due to fans trying to break down Beatles' lyrics.

Since the title of the album, *Sgt. Pepper's Lonely Hearts Club Band*, containing the word "pepper," we decided to create a recipe focused heavily on peppers; therefore, the pepper dip came to life.

SOUNDING SEA SNAPPER

> "And so, all the night-tide, I lie down by the side
> Of my darling — my darling —
> my life and my bride,
> In her sepulchre there by the sea —
> In her tomb by the sounding sea."
>
> *"Annabel Lee"* - 1849

INGREDIENTS

1 teaspoon italian lemon olive oil

2 tablespoons soy sauce

1 tablespoon honey ginger balsamic vinegar

1 tablespoons asian seasoning

1 tablespoon garlic, minced

¼ teaspoon paprika

1/8 teaspoon cayenne pepper

1 lb. red snapper filet

*lb.- pound, *Tbsp - tablespoon, *tsp - teaspoon

INSTRUCTIONS

Preheat the oven to 375°F. Mix together all liquid ingredients and spices. Place the red snapper into a gallon size resealable bag and pour the mixture over the red snapper. Seal the bag airtight. Marinade filets in mixture for 10-15 minutes in the refrigerator. Place the snapper filets in a baking dish or on a rimmed baking sheet to cook. Bake for 20 minutes, until the snapper easily flakes with a fork.

Inspiration

Another Poe favorite, "Annabel Lee," has been adapted several times in music. One such time was in 2011 by none other than Stevie Nicks released on her album, *In Your Dreams*. Her version is absolutely beautiful and she only has minor changes in the lyrics to work with the music. Again, this is just another masterful job of keeping Poe in pop culture and relevant. We wanted to honor this Poe classic with a dish oozing out of the ocean, or sea, since the setting is a kingdom by the sea. We felt a red snapper entree with "snap" to the beat, with honeyed words and a peppery finish.

FOLLOWING THE BACON CUPCAKES

> "The end of the Poe cult cannot be foretold. It has not reached its height."
>
> *Eugene L. Didier, "The Poe Cult," Bookman: A Magazine of Literature and Life, (New York, NY), December 1902*

INGREDIENTS

- 2 2/3 Cups All Purpose Flour
- 2 Cups Sugar
- 1 Tbsp Baking Soda
- 3/4 tsp Salt
- 2/3 Cup Bacon Drippings
- 1 Tbsp Maple Syrup
- 6 Tbsp Butter, softened
- 6 Egg Whites
- 1 Cup Milk
- 1/2 Cup Bacon, chopped

INSTRUCTIONS

Cook bacon how you prefer-fried in pan on burner or baked in oven-as directed on package, placing bacon on paper towels after it is cooked dabbing off the excess grease. (Save bacon grease from pan it was cooked in) Let bacon grease cool, but do not let it solidify. Mix flour, sugar, soda, and salt in a bowl. While bacon grease cools, press a paper towel to remove more grease from bacon. Chop bacon into small bit size pieces. In a separate bowl, beat egg whites and butter until creamy. Add milk, maple syrup, and bacon grease (if the bacon grease is not 2/3 a cup, use vegetable oil to make up the rest), continuing to mix. Add dry ingredients a little at a time, using the mixer, until all combined. Spoon in bacon bits and stir into cake batter. Bake for 17-20 minutes at 350 degrees. Cool cupcakes, then ice, placing icing into a frosting bag.

Maple Cocoa Icing

3 Cups Powdered Sugar
1 Stick Butter, softened
1 tsp Maple Syrup
2 tsp Cocoa Powder
1/4 Cup Heavy Cream
Pinch of salt

In a bowl, add butter, maple syrup, cocoa powder, and salt and mix until creamy. Add Heavy Cream and mix until blended. Add powdered sugar a little at a time, beating with mixer until creamy and eventually all powdered sugar is added.

Inspiration

The inspiration for this recipe comes from the TV show, *The Following*, starring Kevin Bacon. The show rand from 2013-15. Bacon plays an FBI agent trying to catch a cult leader who just happens to be an English professor obsessed with Edgar Allan Poe. The first episode will have you reeling at the sight of many "Poes" running around. We thought adding this recipe adapted from this show would be a nice modern Pop Culture connection, especially because this gives us the excuse to use bacon as an ingredient. When you make these, be ready for bacon dreaminess.

CHAPTER

THREE

THE GOLD-BUG

> "During this colloquy no portion of Jupiter's person could be seen; but the beetle, which he had suffered to descend, was now visible at the end of the string, and glistened, like a globe of burnished gold, in the last rays of the setting sun, some of which still faintly illumined the eminence upon which we stood."
>
> *The Gold-Bug - 1843*

INGREDIENTS

2 oz. Chardonnay (Wine)

1 oz. White Rum (Real McCoy suggested)

½ oz. Orange Liqueur

½ oz. Demerara Simple Syrup

Old Bay Seasoning

INSTRUCTIONS

Line the rim of the glass with lemon or lime juice. Pour a pile of Old Bay Seasoning on a plate. Roll the rim in the Old Bay. Pour the ingredients in a shaker tin with ice and shake until chilled. Strain the cocktail into the rimmed glass.

Inspiration

Jeff and Carmen visited all of the Poe places at Fort Moultrie and Charleston, some built on local legends and some quite interesting. One of the delicious meals many restaurants serve in the Charleston, S. C. area is a low-country boil. After trying several of the shrimp boils, they discovered they were milder, but more buttery than the cajun styles they were accustomed to eating in other states. On one of their last days in Charleston, they went to the Charleston Crab House for lunch. They asked the waiter what the difference in the boils was because they were a little more unique. The waiter explained that more butter is added to the boil, but the Old Bay seasoning and other spices were present just like in other types of boils.

Jeff and Carmen decided they wanted to pay homage to Poe and their trip to Charleston by creating a gold cocktail to represent the Gold-Bug. Not only did they want the color to be gold, but they wanted to recreate the buttery taste of the boil, including the Old Bay seasoning. They went through many iterations of rums and other liquors until realizing a Chardonnay wine has the perfect buttery note they were looking for as a key ingredient. Jeff mixed the ingredients in this recipe, lined the rim with Old Bay, and the Gold-Bug was born.

History

Poe joined the army in 1827 under the alias Edgar Perry. He was stationed in Fort Moultrie, South Carolina, right outside of Charleston. His experiences during his time in the army at Fort Moultrie provided him the insight to write his short story, The Gold-Bug.

EYE OF THE SKULL

> "Pay attention, then! – find the left eye of the skull."
>
> *The Gold-Bug - 1843*

INGREDIENTS

½ oz. Lemon Juice

1 oz. Demerara Simple Syrup

¾ oz. Aged Dominican Rum

½ oz. Clement Creole Shrubb

¼ oz. Allspice Dram

1 ½ oz. Strongly brewed Peach Tea

INSTRUCTIONS

Mix all ingredients over ice in a mixing tin until the tin is frosty. Pour into a skull mug and garnish with mint and a gold-bug, if you can borrow it from Legrand.

History & Inspiration 50

For this cocktail, we went with a standard rum punch recipe: three of Strong (Rum, Shrubb, and Dram), four of Weak (Peach Tea), two of Sweet (Demerara Simple Syrup), and one of Sour (Lemon Juice). However, we adapted the recipe to balance the drink.

The origins of rum punch go back to the 1630s where the Hindi word "panch" meant five; thus, five ingredients: citrus, spice, spirit, sugar, and water. Officers of the East India Company and British merchants preferred a punch over beer and wine because the punch was more refreshing and preserved better than the other choices. These British sailors brought back these recipes to their homeland where punches are still being served all across the world.

Poe's story, *The Gold-Bug*, is filled with adventure and a sense of detective fiction; however, we added it under our degree of Science/SciFi due to the cryptogram Poe includes in the story for the narrator and Legrand to decipher. The inspiration for this cocktail comes from the part of the story when Jupiter, directed by Legrand, climbs up a particular tree, finds the branch with a skull nailed to it, and drops the gold-bug through the eye of the skull in order to find the buried treasure.

A THOUSAND-AND-SECOND POMEGRANATE MARGARITA OF SCHEHERAZADE

"Sinbad went on, in this manner, with his narrative to the caliph — 'I thanked the man-animal for its kindness, and soon found myself very much at home on the beast, which swam at a prodigious rate through the ocean; although the surface of the latter is, in that part of the world, by no means flat, but round like a pomegranate, so that we went — so to say — either up hill or down hill all the time.'"

A Thousand-and-Second Tale of Scheherazade - 1845

INGREDIENTS

2 oz. Tequila

1/2 oz. Pomegranate juice

1 oz. Lime juice

1/2 oz. Orange Liquor

1/4 oz. Rich simple syrup

INSTRUCTIONS

Put ingredients in a mixing tin, add ice, shake until the tin is cold. Strain into a coupe glass. Garnish with lime wheel.

Inspiration 52

In Poe's satirical/scientific tale, *A Thousand-and-Second Tale of Sheherazade*, he tells of a king who was betrayed by his wife and has her executed. He vows to wed and execute a new bride each day. Scheherazade is the next bride. To extend her life, she starts to tell the king stories, but leaves them unfinished each night where the king wants to hear the end of the tales the next day. These tales are based on Sinbad's tales, but contain modern inventions from the 19th century. This cocktail was inspired by the mention of pomegranate and how nice it could be added to a traditional margarita.

THE BALLOON HOAX HASHBROWNS

> "We have crossed the Atlantic — fairly and easily crossed it in a balloon! God be praised! Who shall say that anything is impossible hereafter? ——"
>
> *The Balloon Hoax - 1844*

INGREDIENTS

2 Large Sweet Potatoes, peeled and shredded

1/2 Cup Brown Sugar

1 tsp Nutmeg

2 tsp Cinnamon

1/2 Stick Butter

*lb.- pound, *Tbsp - tablespoon, *tsp - teaspoon

INSTRUCTIONS

Peel and shred the sweet potatoes and place in a large mixing bowl.

In a small mixing bowl, mix together brown sugar, nutmeg, and cinnamon. Remove as many clumps in the brown sugar as you can. A fork may be the best way to mash the clumps up. Place spice mixture in bowl of shredded potatoes to coat as you mix it up. Heat up the skillet, placing 1/4 stick of butter to melt. Once melted, place potatoes in a skillet, stir to mix and coat, chop remaining 1/4 cup of butter into slices. Stir into the potatoes. Cook until potatoes are cooked all the way through.

Inspiration

In 1844, in the New York Sun, *The Balloon Hoax*, was published as a factual account of adventurers led by Mr. Monck Mason on a transatlantic voyage from England. The story gave detailed accounts of the mechanics of the balloon as it only took three days to conduct this voyage. Poe's hoax was a precursor to Orson Welles performing *War of the Worlds* on the radio in 1938. Since the story was actually fictional, we thought about hashbrowns for the recipe to honor this story. However, to create the "hoax," we changed the potatoes from white to sweet to provide you with a scrumptious deviation on a classic breakfast staple.

HANS PFAALL'S LEMON POPPYSEED MUFFINS

> "Then I came suddenly into still noonday solitudes, where no wind of heaven ever intruded, and where vast meadows of poppies, and slender, lily-looking flowers spread themselves out a weary distance, all silent and motionless for ever."
>
> *The Unparalleled Adventure of One Hans Pfaaall - 1835*

INGREDIENTS

1 3/4 cups all purpose flour

1/4 cup sugar

2 tsp. Baking powder

1/2 tsp Salt

1 egg, beaten

1/2 cup milk

1/4 lemon juice

1/3 cup Cooking oil

1 Tbsp. Poppy Seeds

1/8 - 1/4 tsp. Lemon zest

INSTRUCTIONS

Preheat the oven to 400 degrees. Add cupcake liners to a cupcake/muffin pan. Mix dry ingredients together: flour, sugar, baking powder, and salt leaving a well in the middle. Combine the egg, milk, lemon juice, cooking oil, poppy seeds, and lemon zest. Add the wet mixture to the center of the dry mixture and stir together until it is moist and the batter is lumpy. Spoon ⅔ cup of batter into each cupcake liner. Bake at 400 degrees for around 10-15 minutes or until golden. Allow muffins to cool slightly before adding the glaze. Yields 10 to 12 muffins.

*lb.- pound, *Tbsp - tablespoon, *tsp - teaspoon

Lemon Glaze

1 Cup Powdered sugar
2 Tbsp. Lemon Juice

Mix the powdered sugar and lemon juice together until blended. Drizzle over cooled muffins. Serve when muffins are just slightly warm.

Inspiration

The Unparalleled Adventure of One, Hans Pfaall is a science fiction tale written by Poe in 1835. Hans Pfaall needs to escape his creditors and abysmal life, so he creates a balloon that will take him to the moon and a device to help him breathe. The trip takes him 19 days where he reaches the moon finding a city with inhabitants. A messenger is sent back to his planet with a note to exchange information about the moon for forgiveness of Pfaall's crime. We chose Lemon Poppyseed Muffins for this story because poppies are mentioned in Poe's sci/fi tale. Bake these up, brew some tea, and read this satirically scientific tale.

EUREKA! IT'S ORANGE!

> "Now, if the orange be understood as the Sun, and the pea as a planet revolving about it, then the revolution should be made at such a rate — with a velocity so varying — that the radius vector may pass over equal areas of space in equal times."
>
> *"Eureka: A Prose Poem"* - 1848

INGREDIENTS

Honey Graham Cracker Crust *
1 sleeve of Honey Graham Crackers finely crushed
1/2 cup Walnuts, chopped
1/4 c. granulated sugar
8 Tbsp. butter, melted
Pinch salt

Orange Pudding **
2 3/4 cups whole milk (1/4 cup will be used for mixing with the cornstarch)
1/4 Orange Liqeuer
4 tablespoons cornstarch
Pinch of salt
¾ cup sugar
3 egg yolks
1 tablespoon butter
2 teaspoons orange extract

*lb.- pound, *Tbsp - tablespoon, *tsp - teaspoon

INSTRUCTIONS

*Mix ingredients together, pour into 9x13 baking dish, press the crust down evenly across the dish. Bake in 350 degree oven for 10-12 minutes.

** In a small bowl, whisk together ¼ cup of the milk with the cornstarch. Set aside.

In a medium saucepan, whisk together the remaining 2 1/2 cups milk, orange liqeuor, salt, and sugar. Cook over medium heat until it is steaming; however, do not let it boil.

While the milk mixture heats, whisk the egg yolks in a separate small bowl. Once the milk mixture is steaming, remove a 1/2 cup of the hot milk mixture and slowly pour it into the bowl with the egg yolks, whisking constantly. Slowly add the egg yolk mixture back to the saucepan, then add the cornstarch mixture. Continue to cook over medium heat, whisking constantly, until the mixture starts to simmer and has thickened. Remove from the heat and whisk in the butter and orange extract.

Constructing It

1 block of cream cheese, sit out for several hours until soft
1 - 16 oz. container of whipped topping
1 - 15 oz. can of mandarin oranges, drained
Rest of 8 oz. package of walnuts

In a bowl, mix together the cream cheese and half of a 16 oz. container of whipped topping. Drain the can of mandarin oranges and mix into the cream cheese and whipped topping mixture. In the 9x13 pan with the graham cracker/walnut crust, which should be cooled, add a layer of the cream cheese mixture over the graham cracker crust; next, add the orange pudding mixture over the top, add another layer of the cream cheese mixture next; then add the other half of the whipped topping onto the last layer of the cream cheese mixture. Sprinkle the rest of the walnuts on top of the dessert. Place in the refrigerator for several hours before serving.

Inspiration

Poe's "Eureka: A Prose Poem" is his scientific theory he wrote about based on the universe beginning from one specific point of matter where everything is interconnected. There is much more to this work, but there is too much to go into in our recipe book. Therefore, we chose this dessert based on orange being mentioned in his work. Additionally, Poe's Eureka has many layers to read through, so this dessert also provides many layers for you to enjoy.

MELLONTA FLAUTAS

> "The worm was carefully fed on mulberries — a kind of fruit resembling a water-melon — and, when sufficiently fat, was crushed in a mill. The paste thus arising was called papyrus in its primary state, and went through a variety of processes until it finally became 'silk'."
>
> *Mellonta Tauta - 1849*

INGREDIENTS

1 lb. Watermelon, chopped in small pieces

1/2 cup water

1/2 cup sugar

1/8 cup cornstarch

1/2 tsp vanilla extract

Package of flour street taco sized tortillas

Cinnamon and brown sugar for sprinkling inside tortilla shells.

INSTRUCTIONS

Place watermelon, sugar, cornstarch, and vanilla extract in a small sauce pan. Add water last. Cook a little bit higher than medium, but not on high until boiling, stirring until boiling where the mixture thickens to a nice pie filling consistency.

Brush inside tortilla with oil and sprinkle with cinnamon and brown sugar; add no more than two Tbsp. of watermelon mixture to center; roll up sticking a toothpick in middle turning where the tortilla meets on bottom. Lightly brush tops with oil. Bake at 375 degrees for ten-12 minutes (Pre-heat oven before baking). Makes around 24 Flautas.

Inspiration

Mellonta Tauta written in 1849 is a satirical and science fiction short story told by the narrator, Pundit. Pundit goes on a balloon trip to space in the year 2848 and he gives details of his journey and what he encounters. With the help of Jeff's daughter Sydney and her husband Josh, who came up with the name for this recipe, Mellonta Flautas, a watermelon flauta was born. The decision to use watermelon came from the quote we used and with the play on words of Mellonta to Melon, it worked perfectly.

HORROR 6º

CHAPTER

FOUR

MONTRESOR'S REVENGE

"The thousand injuries of Fortunato I had borne as I best could, but when he ventured upon insult I vowed revenge."

The Cask of Amontillado - 1846

INGREDIENTS

1 oz. Amontillado Sherry

1 oz. Amaro Montenegro

1/2 oz. Angostura Bitters

2 Dashes Fee Brothers Aztec Chocolate Bitters

INSTRUCTIONS

Put ingredients into a mixing glass with ice, stir with a bar spoon until the outside of the glass is chilled, strain into a coupe glass.

History

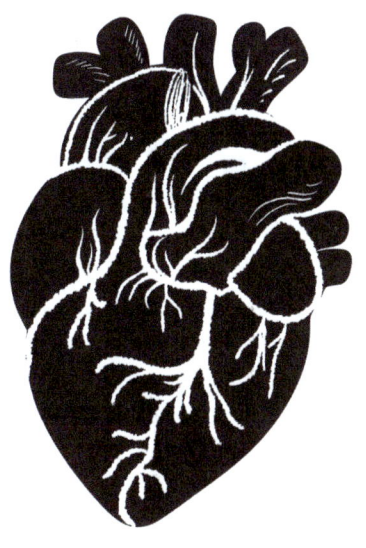

The Cask of Amontillado is a favorite short story among the three of us; therefore, we felt it would be a faux pas to not create a cocktail for the ultimate murderer, Montressor. In the beginning of the story, Montressor does not give a specific reason for his revenge, except that Fortunato insulted Montressor's family name. He premeditated, luring Fortunato down to the catacombs to his untimely death all in the name of an Amontillado. Unfortunately for Fortunato, he fell for it.

Inspiration

The main ingredient of the cocktail is, of course, an Amontillado Sherry, with other ingredients to balance out the taste of revenge. The Amaro Montenegro adds a sweet and bitter combination while the two bitters also add a sweet and bitter combination with a little chocolate spice. Once these ingredients are melded together with ice, as the old adage (This saying was first introduced in Eugène Sue's novel Memoirs of Matilda in 1846) says, "Revenge is a dish best served cold."

THE LAST JEST

> "As for myself, I am simply Hop-Frog, the jester — and this is my last jest."
>
> *Hop-Frog - 1849*

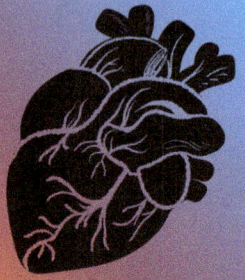

INGREDIENTS

1 1/2 oz Tequila

1 1/2oz Grape juice

1oz Lemon

1/2oz Orgeat

1/2oz BG Reynolds Paradise Blend

1/2 oz Ancho Reyes Liqueur

Cinnamon/Nutmeg Spice Mix

INSTRUCTIONS

Put ingredients into a mixing tin over ice, shake until the outside of the tin is very cold to the touch, strain into a tiki mug. Place a spent lemon shell on top with a sugar cube soaked in lemon extract. Light on fire. To add zest to the fire, shake cinnamon/nutmeg spice mix over the fire. Blow the fire out before drinking.

Inspiration

The inspiration to create this cocktail came from a tiki cocktail contest for the tiki festival, Ohana! Luau at the Lake in 2024 with tequila being the one required ingredient. So, Jeff and Carmen utilized elements from another story of revenge, *Hop-Frog*. Since the king and his men were drinking wine, grape juice was chosen; furthermore, the story brings on a strong element of fire, so Ancho Reyes Liqueur was used, along with lighting the drink on fire at the end. The name of the cocktail comes from the quote listed under the cocktail name. Hop-frog is simply a jester; however, his Last Jest is full of wrath and fire.

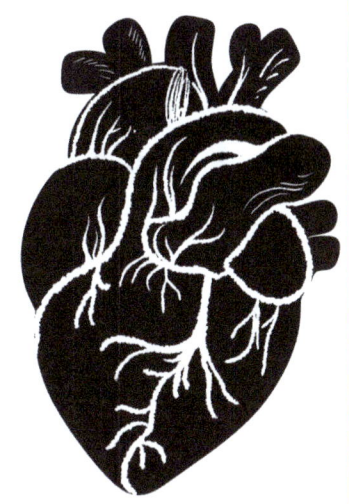

THE TELL-TALE HEART

> "Villains!" I shrieked, "dissemble no more! I admit the deed! — tear up the planks! — here, here! — it is the beating of his hideous heart!"
>
> *The Tell-Tale Heart - 1843*

INGREDIENTS

1 Maraschino Cherry

1-2 Dashes Fee Brother's Aztec Chocolate Bitters

Glass of Champagne or Prosecco

INSTRUCTIONS

Mash Maraschino cherry just enough to split open inside the champagne flute. Add a few dashes of the Fee Brother's Aztec chocolate bitters. Fill either Champagne or Prosecco almost to the top of the flute.

Inspiration

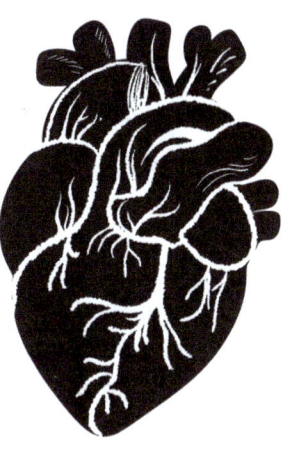

Driven mad with the idea of always being watched, always being scrutinized leads to the breaking point of a caregiver. Poe takes us into the psychological downfall of the unnamed narrator in this tale, driving suspense every minute to the very end of the story.

Experimenting with a cocktail to dedicate to this short story, we wanted to create some type of beating heart even however difficult. Once we added the cherry to the bottom of the champagne flute and poured champagne over it, nothing really happened except for the bubbles; however, when we smashed the cherry ever so lightly, adding the bitter, and then poured the champagne on top, the cherry gave the appearance of moving, as if beating, from the effervescent bubbles.

THE PIT AND THE PENDULUM CHARCUTERIE

> "Upon my recovery, too, I felt very — oh, inexpressibly sick and weak, as if through long inanition. Even amid the agonies of that period, the human nature craved food."
>
> *The Pit and the Pendulum - 1842*

INGREDIENTS

Green and/or Black Olives

Pretzel Sticks

Cheese

(Variety of your choice)

INSTRUCTIONS

The olives are the Pit. The pretzels are the stick part of the Pendulum. The cheese is the blade of the Pendulum.

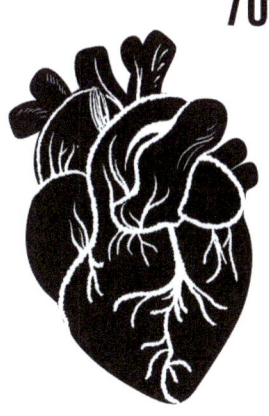

Inspiration

Sometimes in our life we are stuck between a rock and a hard place, much like the poor soul in this story. He finds himself in the midst of punishment we do not know he committed. He is being disciplined through tortuous means. The agony of being left in a pit waiting for what is to come is psychologically devastating paired with the hunger resulting in delirium; later, only to find himself awaiting the pendulum sharpened with great care descending upon him.

The reading of this story has you reaching for comfort as the agony of the character facing certain doom. When we discussed the elements of the story, we felt like a charcuterie would represent the name and offer sustenance as an appetizer. The pit naturally caused us to think of the pimento pits in olives, adding them to the center as a circular pit as in the story. To create the pendulum, we felt the pretzel sticks with the cheese as the blade complemented the pit.

THE DEVILED EGGS IN THE BELFRY

> "Affairs being thus miserably situated, I left the place in disgust, and now appeal for aid to all lovers of good time and fine kraut."
>
> *The Devil in the Belfry - 1839*

INGREDIENTS

½ Eggs (Hardboiled)

2 Tbsp. Miracle Whip

1 Tbsp. Sugar

1 Tbsp. Mustard

¼ Cup Spicy Maple Bourbon Pickles*

*Salt and Pepper to taste

Paprika for garnish

INSTRUCTIONS

Remove yolks from egg whites and mash. Mix with all ingredients. Carefully spoon egg yolk mixture into the egg whites. Sprinkle paprika on top of each deviled egg. *Pickles from Walmart.

*lb.- pound, *Tbsp - tablespoon, *tsp - teaspoon

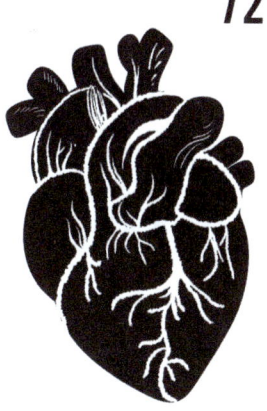

Inspiration

Many a time we have all come across a prankster, an imp, or simply what we call a little devil, which is what Poe gives us in the story, *The Devil in the Belfry*. He tells a tale of the woes that many, especially the animals, have to endure because of the one prankster that no one adores.

Using inspiration from the story, the recipe of deviled eggs fit most appropriately by boiling, cracking, ejecting, and smashing, you take your vexation from the little imp in the story into your recipe. By mixing the ingredients, along with the addition of some fiery taste. You get the jist of the story through more than one sense.

THE CHICKEN OF AMONTILLADO

> "Enough," he said; "the cough is a mere nothing; it will not kill me. I shall not die of a cough."
>
> *The Cask of Amontillado - 1846*

INGREDIENTS

6 chicken tenderloins
1 tsp Salt
1 tsp White pepper
1 tsp Minced Garlic
1 tsp Basil
1 tsp Rosemary
1 tsp Thyme
1 tsp Oregano
1 tsp Parsley
1/4 cup All Purpose Flour
1/2 cup Amontillado
1/4 cup Cooking Sherry
4 Tbsp Butter
4 Tbsp Olive oil
1/4 cup diced Onion
12 pieces cut up Asparagus
1 package Cherry Tomatoes
6 Sweet peppers, sliced, removing all seeds and pulp from inside each pepper
Half and half

*lb.- pound, *Tbsp - tablespoon, *tsp - teaspoon

INSTRUCTIONS

Mix dry spices with flour and coat tenderloins. Melt butter and olive oil in a pan, add chicken, garlic, onion. Cook chicken until brown. Add Amontillado, cooking Sherry, cherry tomatoes, and sweet peppers. Cover, cook for 5 minutes, turn chicken, cook for five minutes more. Check chicken temperature with a thermometer, making sure the chicken is at 165 degrees.

You may add the Asparagus in when you add the tomatoes and peppers (they will cook well, but will not be as crunchy); however, you may add a little olive oil to a small skillet with a pinch of salt, white pepper, and garlic powder. Cook until a tiny bit brown and crunchy. Add the Asparagus to the dish.

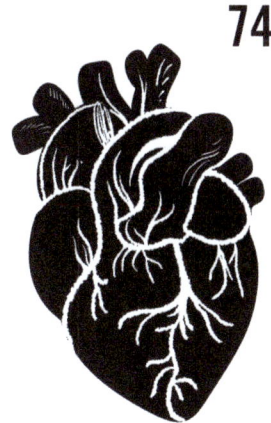

Inspiration

For the Chicken of Amontillado, we decided on a play on words for this recipe. However, we added amontillado as one of the ingredients to add to the sense of Poe's short story. If Montressor was planning to give Fortunato one last meal; hopefully, it would be this delicious dish.

NEVER BET THE DEVIL YOUR OLIVES

> "She did her best in the way of flogging him while an infant — for duties to her well-regulated mind were always pleasures, and babies, like tough steaks, or the modern Greek olive trees, are invariably the better for beating — but, poor woman!"

Never Bet the Devil Your Head - 1841

INGREDIENTS

5 chicken tenderloins
1 can black olives, sliced or diced, and drained
5 Sweet Peppers, deseeded and diced
1 pack Cherry Tomatoes, cut in halves
1/4 Cup Onion, diced
1 tsp Salt
1 tsp White Pepper
2 tsp Paprika
2 tsp Garlic Powder
1 Tbsp Italian Seasoning
1 Tbsp Olive Oil
1/8 Cup Balsamic Vinegar
1/4 Cup Red Wine - Merlot
1-2 Tbsp Brown Sugar (add more or less for level of sweetness)
1 box Pasta (Bowtie was used for this recipe, but you can choose your preference)

*lb.- pound, *Tbsp - tablespoon, *tsp - teaspoon

INSTRUCTIONS

Cut the chicken in small bite size portions. Add olive oil to a skillet and warm for just a minute. Add the chicken, the diced onion, the diced sweet peppers, salt, garlic powder, and pepper. Cook until the chicken is cooked through and tender; the onion will be translucent. Cook your pasta while this is cooking.

Add the halved cherry tomatoes, olives, paprika, italian seasoning, brown sugar, balsamic vinegar, and red wine. Let this simmer on a lower temperature until the tomatoes are tender-around 10-15 minutes. Check for taste and add a little more brown sugar if you desire a sweeter flavor. Once the noodles are cooked, drain the noodles, add a light coating of olive oil to the noodles. Plate pasta with the chicken mixture over the pasta. Serve with a little parmesan cheese for garnish.

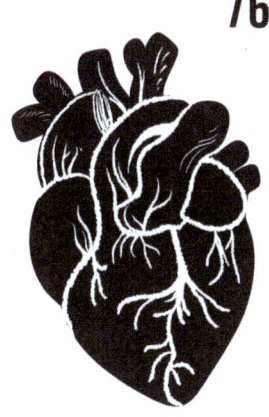

Inspiration

This recipe has two styles of inspiration: a play on words and one of the ingredients is actually mentioned in the short story. We started with the mention of olives and then thinking in a pun-state of mind, we came up with the name Never Bet the Devil Your Olives. Ironically, an olive is kind of in the shape of a head. Carmen created this recipe long before the thought of this recipe book, and she was all too ecstatic to share it as a Poe-themed recipe celebrating the story's main character, Toby Dammit. He continuously bet the devil his head one too many times.

THE OBLONG BOX OF GREEN TEACAKES

> "I repeat, therefore, that it must have been, simply, a freak of my own fancy, distempered by good Captain Hardy's green tea."
>
> *The Oblong Box - 1844*

INGREDIENTS

4 cups self rising flour

2 eggs

2 cups granulated sugar

1/2 stick butter, melted

1/4 cup shortening

1/2 cup buttermilk

1/2 tsp pure vanilla extract

1/2 tsp lemon juice

1/4 tsp Nutmeg

Zest from 1 lemon

*Tbsp - tablespoon, *tsp - teaspoon

INSTRUCTIONS

Preheat oven to 400 degrees. Grease two cookie sheets. In a large bowl, sift flour and then add sugar. Add the shortening, taking a fork to smooth it out when mixing. In a separate medium sized bowl, whisk melted butter, buttermilk, vanilla extract, eggs (make sure the melted butter is cooled off before adding the eggs) lemon juice, lemon zest, and nutmeg until smooth.

Pour wet ingredients into dry and mix until combined. Do not mix too long so the dough will not be overworked. Place either parchment paper or wax paper down on the counter. Add light flour to your papered counter and turn out dough. Roll out the dough with light pressure to around a 1/4 of inch thickness (the thinner the dough, the crispier the teacake). I only did small parts of the dough at a time so I would not overwork the dough. Take your favorite cookie cutters and cut out your teacakes placing each one about 3/4" to 1" apart on your cookie sheets. If you want to keep to tradition, use a round cookie cutter. Bake for 6-8 minutes or until lightly browned.

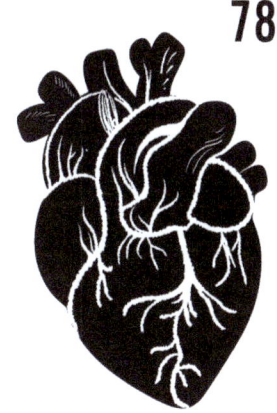

Teacake Glaze

4 cups powdered sugar, sifted
4 tablespoons honey
4 tablespoons buttermilk
4 tablespoons green tea, cooled
Green food coloring, optional

After sifting the powdered sugar, mix the rest of the ingredients together. The glaze will have a thick consistency like a liquid frosting. After your teacakes are cooled off, spread the glaze over each teacake, not too thick. The glaze will not appear smooth; however, it will smooth out beautifully and harden (not crispy).

Note: If you want to use a different kind of tea, you may substitute the same amount for the green tea. You may also use a different color of food coloring.

Inspiration

These are best paired with a hot cup of any kind of tea.

Teacakes and scones are similar, but different; however, many use the names interchangeably. In Poe's short story, *The Oblong Box*, not only was tea mentioned, but green tea. This gave us a jumpstart on creating teacakes using green tea. Teacakes' history began sometime before the Revolutionary War and connected to African American culture. Have yourself a cup of green tea while you eat one of these tantalizing teacakes.

SURREALISM 60

CHAPTER

FIVE

DREAM WITHIN A DREAMSICLE

> "*All* that we see or seem is but a dream within a dream."
>
> "A Dream Within a Dream" - 1849

INGREDIENTS

1 Chocolate Kiss

2 oz. Orange Liqueur

2 oz. Half and Half

INSTRUCTIONS

Add the Hershey's Kiss to the bottom of the glass you will serve the drink in. Add both ingredients to a tin or mixing glass with a few ice cubes. Stir, do not shake, and pour over the kiss in a coupe or martini glass.

Inspiration

Poe's poem, "Dream Within a Dream," epitomizes surrealism for the speaker of the poem pondering whether the dream is reality or further subconscious in his or her brain, such as the line, "All that we see or seem/Is but a dream within a dream." For this cocktail, we wanted to incorporate that surrealistic feeling of a dream-like state. Adding the chocolate kiss at the bottom of the glass brings about this notion because the flavor of an orange dreamsicle is sweet and delectable; however, when one arrives at the end with the chocolate flavor added to the orange flavor, the surrealism comes out because it is not expected. The chocolate kiss becomes the dream within a dream.

ISLAND OF THE "FAY" LARNUM

> "If ever island were enchanted," — said I to myself, — "this is it..."
>
> *The Island of the Fay - 1841*

INGREDIENTS

2 oz. Mandarin orange juice

1/2 oz. Lemon

1 oz. Falernum

1 oz. Dr. Byrd Pineapple Rum

1/2 oz. Demerara Rum

Bar spoon of Tiki Bitters

INSTRUCTIONS

Add all ingredients to a mixing tin. Shake over ice and pour into a mai tai glass and top with ice. Garnish with a spent mandarin orange half and mint.

Inspiration

Poe's work, *The Island of the Fay,* is an allegorical tale with a fairy moving around a mysterious island. Elements he incorporated were physical and spiritual realms, a light and dark side to the island, nature, and death. The fairy fades, moving to the darker side of the island.

For this cocktail, we decided to go with the play on words or the name with a focus on the word "fay" and the focus on the ingredient "falernum." Ultimately, we mixed the two words together creating The Island of the "Fay"lernum. With the setting for this piece being set on an island, we went with a tiki styled cocktail; moreover, falernum is a common tiki cocktail ingredient.

ELDORADO OLD FASHIONED

> "Over the Mountains
> Of the Moon,
> Down the Valley of the Shadow,
> Ride, boldly ride,"
> The shade replied, —
> "If you seek for Eldorado!"
>
> *Eldorado - 1849*

INGREDIENTS

2 oz. Eldorado 8 Year Demerara Rum

1 Barspoonful full of rich Demarara Simple Syrup

1/2 Barspoonful Bitterman's Burlesque Bitters

1/2 Barspoonful Allspice Bitters

INSTRUCTIONS

Use a rocks glass to build the cocktail in the glass. Add each ingredient over ice (preferably, over one large cube). Once all ingredients are in the glass, stir the cocktail until ingredients are mixed together.

History

To seek that fortune, one must set upon the impossible journey. As children, we all seek that gold at the end of a rainbow and Poe's poem gives us the quest, but unfortunately, never reaching the end of the rainbow.

Inspiration

To honor this cocktail, we thought it very fitting to use the Eldorado 8 Year Demerara Rum paired with the necessary ingredients for an Old Fashioned. The richer simple syrup created from Demarara sugar reflects the richness of the poem that is being sought and to savor. The bitters in the cocktail represent the trials and tribulations of the obstacles the rider went through in seeking Eldorado.

GOLDEN SAND BISCUITS

> "I stand amid the roar
> Of a surf-tormented shore,
> And I hold within my hand
> Grains of the golden sand —
> How few! yet how they creep
> Through my fingers to the deep,
> While I weep — while I weep!"

A Dream Within a Dream - 1849

INGREDIENTS

1 ¾ Cups Self Rising Flour

⅔-¾ Cups Milk

⅓ Cup Shortening

1 Cup Shredded Cheddar Cheese

1 ½ Tbsp Dried Chives

½ Tsp Garlic Powder

3 Tbsp Melted Butter

Garlic Salt for sprinkling

INSTRUCTIONS

Mix flour and shortening together. Add cheese, chives, and garlic powder to the flour/shortening mix. Add milk until moistened enough to drop spoonfuls of the mixture onto a cookie sheet. Bake in a pre-heated oven at 400 degrees for 10-15 minutes. Melt a few Tbsp. of butter. Brush melted butter onto cooked biscuits and lightly sprinkle garlic salt on top of biscuits. They are ready to be served.

88

Inspiration

"A Dream Within a Dream" is one of Carmen's favorite poems. The specific line, "Grains of the golden sand," made her think of her cheesy, garlic biscuits. Every time she makes these, they are a hit; you might say golden. Enjoy these biscuits with any of our pasta dishes. They are even tasty eating them as an appetizer with a marinara sauce.

ROSEMARY SLEEPER BEER BREAD

> "The rosemary nods upon the grave;
> The lily lolls upon the wave;"
>
> *The Sleeper - 1841*

INGREDIENTS

3 Cups Self-Rising Flour

1/4 Cup Sugar

1 Tbsp Rosemary

1 tsp Garlic Powder

1 12 oz. Beer

1 Stick Butter (1/2 Cup), Melted

INSTRUCTIONS

Preheat the oven to 375 Degrees. Sift flour. Mix dry ingredients together. Add beer and mix until moist. Turn bread mix into a buttered bread pan. Bake for 50 minutes to one hour. Make sure a toothpick comes out clean from the middle. Bread will be golden brown. Let it sit for around 15-20 minutes. The loaf should come out whole. Slice and serve with a little butter.

Inspiration

For some of our recipes, we focused on what type of ingredients Poe mentions in his poems and stories. We gave this simple beer bread recipe a little twist of rosemary since Poe used this herb growing on a grave in the poem, "The Sleeper." Right out of the oven, this bread smells sweet and herby; just add the butter and it melts in your mouth.

DALI'S DREAM ROLLS

> "From a wild weird clime, that lieth, sublime,
> Out of SPACE — out of TIME."
>
> *Dream-Land - 1844*

INGREDIENTS

1 cup butter
1 tablespoon minced garlic
1 tablespoon fresh lemon juice
1 teaspoon dried chives
1/2 teaspoon ground white pepper
2 tablespoons Fee Brothers Aztec Chocolate Bitters
2 lbs. cooked lobster

INSTRUCTIONS

In a large sauce pan, melt butter and mix in the pre-cooked lobster pieces and stir. Add the spices and cook until the sauce has a nice consistency coating the lobster, which should be around 15 minutes.

Pair Dali's Dream Rolls with Poe's Pan Bread. Placing the Dali's Dream Roll lobster mixture into Poe's Pan Bread creates a delicious variant on the hot, buttery lobster roll from the Northeast.

History & Inspiration

Dali epitomizes the definition of surrealism in his art—a true paragon of the movement. From his own artwork to a collaboration with Alfred Hitchcock on the movie *Spellbound*, Dali was a surrealistic genius. He even had a dream about Edgar Allan Poe, inspiring him; therefore, what better person to name a recipe after for our surrealism chapter, especially since Poe wrote a few works about dreams. We were inspired to create Dali's Dream Rolls as a spin on a lobster roll born in the Northeast. Doing our research, we found that adding chocolate to lobster created a wonderful, rich taste. We created a recipe with the warm lobster roll with butter, but adding the chocolate bitters to savor.

POE'S PAN BREAD

> "...we could not get them to approach several very harmless objects — such as the schooner's sails, an egg, an open book, or a pan of flour."
>
> *The Narrative of Arthur Gordon Pym of Nantucket - 1838*

INGREDIENTS

- 2 Cups All Purpose Flour
- 1 Teaspoon Salt
- 1 Teaspoon Demerara Sugar
- 1 1/2 Teaspoons Baking Powder
- 1 1/2 Teaspoon Spanish Paprika
- 1 1/2 Teaspoon Tajin
- 1/2 Cup Milk
- 1/2 Cup ice cold water
- 1/4 Cup Butter, melted

INSTRUCTIONS

Add the dry ingredients (flour, salt, sugar, baking powder & herbs) to a large mixing bowl. Mix dry ingredients together. Soften butter in a microwave.

Add wet ingredients (milk and melted butter) to the mixing bowl. Stir thoroughly with a large spoon. Hand knead the dough for 1 or 2 minutes in order to create a nice ball of dough. Sprinkle a small amount of flour on a cutting board in order to prevent the dough sticking to the cutting board (when you roll out the dough).

Take a golf ball size chunk of dough and place it on the cutting board. Sprinkle a small amount of flour on top of the dough and the rolling pin. Flatten out dough with the rolling pin into a tortilla size shape roughly about 1/8" high. Add 1 or 2 tablespoons of oil or butter to a frying pan on low/medium heat.

Place the flatbread dough in to the frying pan. Cook one or two at a time, depending on frying pan size. Flip all of the flatbreads every minute in order to prevent burning. When golden brown on both sides, remove from pan. Each pan bread should take around 2-4 minutes. Add another 1 tablespoon of oil or butter to the frying pan when you add new ones to cook. Place the cooked pan bread on a wire rack for cooling. Add Dali's Dream Roll lobster mix on a pan bread and enjoy.

Inspiration

For Dali's Dream Rolls, we decided to add a different type of bread. A true warm lobster roll with butter is lobster placed on a New England style split-top hot dog style bun. Since we changed up the recipe to honor Dali, we decided to use pan bread, originating from Spain. This recipe creates a nice flat bread to hold the lobster mixture with a balance of a little sweet and a little spice to complement the meal.

LIONIZING VELOUTE SAUCE A LA CAULIFLOWER

"There was Fricassée from the Rocher de Cancale. He mentioned Latour, Markbrunnen and Mareschino — Muriton of red tongue, and Cauliflowers with Velouté sauce — veal à la St. Menehoult, Marinade à la St. Florentin, and orange jellies en mosaiques."

Lionizing - 1835

INGREDIENTS

2 tbsp butter

3 tbsp All Purpose Flour

2 Cups Chicken Broth

1/4 tsp sea salt

1/8 tsp White pepper

1 tsp chili powder

1/2 tsp ground cumin

1 head of cauliflower or 1 large bag of precut cauliflower

INSTRUCTIONS

Melt butter over medium low heat. Add flour and whisk until mixture is a paste about 2 minutes. Pour in one cup of stock and whisk until smooth and lump free. Slowly whisk the remaining one cup of stock and add all seasonings. Whisk until all blended. Turn heat up to medium. Watch until sauce comes to low boil (small bubbles come up to surface). Once this occurs, keep whisking sauce for 3 minutes. If you want a thicker sauce, whisk in a little flour into desired consistency.

Cauliflower- Add oil and cauliflower. Cook over medium high heat. Mix together with salt and pepper to taste. Cook until desired consistency is reached.

History & Inspiration

Lionizing is a satirical story about a man who instantly gains fame, however short-lived, by the size of his nose. In the story, the Royal Highness of touch-me-not invites the main character to dinner where one of the dishes is "Cauliflowers with Velouté sauce." Researching velouté sauce recipes, Jeff created his own style to honor Mr. Poe, lionizing the cauliflower.

LEMON HALO ANGEL OF THE ODD CAKE

> "Ah!" said I, "I see how it is. This thing speaks for itself. A natural accident, such as will happen now and then!"
>
> *The Angel of the Odd - 1844*

INGREDIENTS

White cake mix
3/4 cup Limoncello (replaces water in cake mix)
½ cup melted butter
4 egg whites
1 tsp Coconut flavoring
2 cups sweetened flake coconut
Vanilla Buttercream Frosting

INSTRUCTIONS

Preheat the oven to 350 degrees. You will need either two 8" round or one 9x11 cake pan. Blend cake mix, Limoncello, butter, egg whites, and coconut flavoring on low for 2 minutes. Bake for 25-29 minutes. Cool on a wire rack for 15 minutes. After the cake has cooled, ice the cake and then add the coconut to the frosting.

Inspiration

At the beginning of the story, the main character had a big meal. After dinner, he sat down to read and was talking about Curiosities by Griswold, and other works, and it made him feel dumb and he didn't feel he deserved to have a dessert, but he wanted one. This cake transcended him into feeling smart like a scholar, bringing the surrealistic approach of him feeling as if he was someone else entirely on another plane, and deserving of this grande heavenly bliss.

POE PLACES 6°

CHAPTER SIX

A BOSTONIAN

"...We like Boston. We were born there -- and perhaps it is just as well not to mention that we are heartily ashamed of the fact."

Broadway Journal - November 1, 1845

INGREDIENTS

1 1/2 oz. Crown Royal Vanilla

1 oz. Irish Cream

1/2 oz. Mozart Chocolate Dark

INSTRUCTIONS

Add ingredients into a mixing tin, shake over ice, and strain into a coupe. These ingredients blended together brings you a most delightful Boston Creme Pie Dessert Cocktail.

History

Edgar Allan Poe was born in Boston, MA on January 19th, 1809 to parents, David Poe, Jr. and Eliza Arnold Poe who were both actors. They moved around to different cities where they could obtain work; thus, Boston being the city of Poe's birth. Poe was not fond of Boston because of his distaste of the transcendentalist movement where many of the noted authors, such as Ralph Waldo Emerson and Henry David Thoreau to name a few, lived and wrote.

Poe moved to Boston after he left the University of Virginia to gain employment. This is where he published his first volume of verse called Tamerlane and Other Poems in 1827. Instead of using his real name, he published the volume under the pseudonym, A Bostonian. Poe was notorious for using pen names throughout his writing career.

Inspiration

The Boston Cream Pie as we know it was first credited in 1856 to The Parker House Hotel, now The Omni Parker House Hotel in Boston, MA. Many cooks from the New England region during this time frame were exceptional bakers, known for their cakes and pies.

Cookware was a limited commodity, so many cooks used pie tins rather than cake pans because the pie tins were more readily available; hence, answering why the Boston Cream Pie became known as a pie rather than a cake. The end result of this delicious dessert is two layers of sponge cake sandwiching in a layer of custard filled cream topped with a chocolate glaze. While Poe died in 1849, we are not sure if he ever ate a Boston Cream Pie, at least unofficially, since it was not named until 1856, but we pay homage to this classic dessert with our dessert cocktail, A Bostonian.

RICHMOND
POE'S BRIDE

> "Thus, while no single sound too rude,
> Upon thy slumber shall intrude,
> Our thoughts, our souls — O God above!
> In every deed shall mingle, love."
>
> *"Serenade" - 1833*

INGREDIENTS

1 1/2 oz. London Dry Gin

1 oz. White Chocolate Liqueur

1/2 oz. Maraschino Liqueur

INSTRUCTIONS

Add ingredients in a mixing tin over ice. Shake until tin is extremely cold to the touch. Double strain into a glass. Garnish with two premium cocktail Cherries.

History & Inspiration

Edgar and Virginia married on May 16, 1836. We chose a London Dry gin because this style would have existed during the 1830s. Gin distilling had come a long way with the Coffee still invention in 1830. The white chocolate liqueur was chosen to represent Virginia's beautiful pale skin, but also the purity of a bride, even though white wedding gowns did not come into fashion until Queen Victoria wed Prince Albert in 1840. The maraschino liqueur was chosen to represent their love for each other.

RICHMOND

THE HAM THAT WAS USED UP

> "I really do believe you would let me go out without my palate."
>
> *The Man that was used Up - 1839*

INGREDIENTS

6-10 lb spiral sliced Ham

Ham Glaze:
½ cup Evan Williams *BiB Bourbon
½ cup Apple Cider
½ cup Dijon Mustard
½ tsp Ground Cloves
1 ½ tsp Ground Ginger
¾ cup Demerara Sugar

*BiB=Bottle in Bond

INSTRUCTIONS

You may use a ham anywhere from 6-10 lbs and will still have some glaze left over. We used a 10 lb spiral sliced ham placed in at least a 1" deep pan, wrapping foil around it. Cook time is 13 minutes per pound, so cook ham for around 2 ½-3 hours at 425 degrees.

For glaze: Whisk ingredients together. Thirty minutes before the ham is done, brush on glaze. Repeat every 10 minutes.

History & Inspiration

In The Man that was Used Up, Poe includes a narrator who tells the story, where he wants to meet Brevet Brigadier General John A.B.C. Smith, a gallant war hero. He comes to find out that appearances can be deceiving, especially with the general who is almost used up in regard to his body's makeup.

This recipe is another one that was easily created from using a play on words. Poe's story, *The Man that was Used Up*, was easy to change to The Ham that was Used Up. Jeff came up with this sugary, spicy glaze to adorn our Thanksgiving ham last year. Everyone loved it!

ENGLAND

THE MANHATTAN OF THE CROWD

> "He refuses to be alone. He is the man of the crowd. It will be in vain to follow; for I shall learn no more of him, nor of his deeds."
>
> *The Man of the Crowd - 1840*

INGREDIENTS

- 2 oz. Rye Whiskey*
- 1/2 oz. London Dry Gin
- 2 Dashes Angostura Bitters

INSTRUCTIONS

Put ingredients into a mixing glass with ice, stir with a bar spoon until the outside of the glass is chilled, strain into a martini or coupe glass.

*We recommend Sagamore Spirits Rye Whiskey distilled in Baltimore, MD.

History

Poe lived in England from 1815-1820, from the time he was 6 until he was 11. Due to his business interests, John Allan, Poe's foster father, moved his family to England. Poe attended grammar school there before the family moved back to Richmond, VA in 1820.

The Man of the Crowd is a story of a man who sits at a coffee shop at the beginning of the story analyzing all the people he sees. At one point, he sees an older man who is concealing a dagger under his clothes; nevertheless, the man begins to follow the old man who leads the man through all parts of London and into the poorest part of the city. The man tries to enter a gin palace, but the manager says it is closing since it is quite early in the morning. The man ends up in front of the old man, wanting to confront him. The man decides he is a criminal genius and the man of the crowd because he never leaves the crowded streets of London.

Inspiration

We decided on this cocktail due to the easy play on words from *The Man of the Crowd* to The Manhattan of the Crowd. This cocktail is a twist on the drink The Manhattan, using London Dry Gin in order to pay homage to the Gin Palace named in the story.

CHARLESTON

THE BEST PEACH COBBLER I EVER HAD!

> "Peaches were like little green velvet buttons"
>
> The Literati of New York City, Godey's Lady's Book - August 1846

INGREDIENTS

For peach mixture:
5 Peaches, peeled, cored, and sliced (about 4 cups)
3/4 Cup Demerara Sugar
1/4 tsp. Salt

For the Batter:
6 Tbsp Butter
1 Cup All-Purpose Flour
1/2 Cup Granulated Sugar
1/2 Cup Brown Sugar
2 tsp. Baking Powder
1/4 tsp. Salt
3/4 Cup Milk
1-2 Tbsp Ground Cinnamon
1/2 Tbsp Nutmeg
1/4 Tbsp Allspice

INSTRUCTIONS

Preheat the oven to 350 degrees. Slice butter into 6 Tbsp and add to a 9x13 inch baking dish. Place the pan with the butter in the oven while it preheats, allowing the butter to melt. Once melted, remove the pan from the oven.

For the peach mixture:
Add the sliced peaches, sugar, and salt to a saucepan and stir to combine. Cook on medium heat for just a few minutes, until the sugar is dissolved and helps to bring out juices from the peaches. The demerara sugar will create a nice thick syrup with the peaches. Remove from heat setting aside.

For the batter:
In a large bowl, mix together the flour, sugar, baking powder, and salt. Stir in the milk to combine. Pour the mixture into the pan, over the melted butter, smoothing it into an even layer. Do not overmix. Spoon the peaches and juice over the batter. Sprinkle cinnamon, nutmeg, and allspice generously over the top.
Bake at 350 degrees for about 38-40 minutes. Serve warm. Adding a scoop of ice cream is a nice addition to the dessert upon serving.

History & Inspiration

For some, this recipe may not be the best peach cobbler he or she ever had, but for Jeff Bouldin, that was his declaration after taking one bite of Carmen's recipe. Carmen suggested using brown sugar for the peach mixture, but Jeff said try Demerara first to see what it does. So Carmen added the brown sugar to the batter and the Demerara sugar to the peach mixture, and wallah, this peach cobbler recipe came into fruition.

Additionally for some, peaches are more associated with the state of Georgia; however, South Carolina claims the juicy fruit as well. Both states grow similar amounts each year with people from both states liking all of the varieties. Since Edgar Allan Poe never lived in Georgia, we will claim the peach as a cobbler dessert for the Poe Place of South Carolina.

In South Carolina, Fort Moultrie is where Poe was stationed while he was in the army as an enlisted soldier from November 1827 to December 1828. He enlisted as Edgar A. Perry, and spent a short time stationed at Fort Independence in Boston, MA before being sent to Fort Moultrie. Fort Moultrie is located on Sullivan's Island just outside of Charleston, SC and has several Poe tourist experiences to visit, such as the Edgar Allan Poe library, streets named after the author and some of his stories, a Gold-Bug tree, the beach, Poe's Tavern - a Poe themed restaurant with yummy Poe themed cocktails and food, and last, but not least Fort Moultrie.

CHARLESTON

JUPITER'S PEACH SALSA

> "It was about a month after this (and during the interval I had seen nothing of Legrand) when I received a visit, at Charleston, from his man, Jupiter."
>
> *The Gold-Bug - 1843*

INGREDIENTS

2 large Peaches, around 1 lb, peeled and diced
2 Cups Cherry Tomatoes, cut in halves
¾ Cup Onion, diced
¾ Cup Sweet Peppers, seeds and insides removed, diced
3 Tbsp Brown Sugar
2 Tbsp Minced Garlic
1 Tsp Ground Ginger
1 ½ Tsp Salt
¼ Cup White Balsamic Vinegar
⅛ Cup Key Lime Juice

INSTRUCTIONS

Once fruit and vegetables are cut and diced, add spices, then add liquids mixing until all spices have dissolved. Chill in the refrigerator for at least 2 hours before serving with tortilla chips.

Inspiration

To continue the South Carolina peach trend, we decided to add Carmen's peach salsa recipe. Not far from the authors resides Breeden's Orchard, where they grow peaches in the summer and apples in the fall. Carmen loves to create recipes from both fruits, especially recipes based on Poe's works. One extra note Carmen wants to add about the salsa is if you are able to use white peaches, the flavor is spectacular.

THE PHILDELPHIA PRESS

> "Little knots of cherry trees and plum bushes grew in various directions..."
>
> *The Journal of Julius Rodman - 1840*

INGREDIENTS

2 oz London Dry Gin

2 oz Fresh Red Plum Juice*

2 oz Carbonated Water

1 oz Rich Simple Syrup

1 oz Lemon Juice

INSTRUCTIONS

Pour plum juice, simple syrup, lemon juice, and gin into mixing tin. Add ice and shake until tin is frosty on the outside. Strain into a Collins glass, add carbonated water, and top with crushed ice stir/agitate with bar spoon to mix ingredients. Garnish with a lemon.

*If you use black plums, it creates a sweeter drink using the same recipe measurements. To lower the sweetness, you could cut back a little on the simple syrup.

History

Edgar Allan Poe, his wife Virginia, and her mother, his aunt, Maria Clemm, moved to Philadelphia in 1838. Here, Poe wrote some of his most well-known masterpieces, such as "Fall of the House of Usher," "The Murders in the Rue Morgue," "The Mask of the Red Death," "The Black Cat," and "Ligeia." In 1842, his wife, Virginia became ill with tuberculosis. The Poes and Mrs. Clemm moved to New York in 1845.

Inspiration

The inspiration came from the Philadelphia created cocktail called the Clover Club. A group of journalists would meet once a week at the Hotel Bellevue from 1883 to 1897; hence, the cocktail was born. The Clover Club contained an egg white, raspberry syrup, lemon juice, and gin. We pay homage to this cocktail by naming it after the "press" or journalists.

We changed the raspberry to plum and took out the sweet and sour cocktail elements by not using the egg white. Poe had several of his works published in newspapers and magazines, so the Philadelphia Press stands firm on its deadline.

THE PHILDELPHIA SMASH

> "--you and that fellow with the plum-pudding face, as blowed me up about a cask of gin!"
>
> *Peter Snook - October, 1836 - Southern Literary Messenger*

INGREDIENTS

1/2 of a plum, cut into 4 quarters

8-10 mint leaves

1/2 oz maple syrup

2 oz Rye whiskey

INSTRUCTIONS

Put plums into a shaker tin. Muddle until partially smashed. Put mint leaves into tin with plums and muddle at least ten times.

Pour maple syrup and Rye whiskey on top of muddled plums and mint. Put ice in tin and shake until the tin is chilled. Strain into a rocks glass over fresh ice. Garnish with a mint sprig.

History & Inspiration

A "smash" style cocktail originates from the julep family of cocktails as early as 1862; however, in 1888, the smash became separated from the julep family with a basic formula of ice, sugar, mint, water, whiskey, and fruit. Plums may be grown in Pennsylvania with the proper understanding of the state's climate conditions and the right plum tree variety. So, we decided a plum smash cocktail was perfect.

A PREDICAMENT'S PHILLY CHEESESTEAK SOUP

> "I told him I would be tender of his feelings — ossi tender que beefsteak."
>
> *A Predicament - 1838*

INGREDIENTS

- 2 lbs Ribeye with chunks of fat trimmed,
- 1 onion diced
- 3 green bell peppers diced
- 4 cups beef broth
- 1 10 oz can beef consomme
- 1 Tbsp Better Than Bullion Roasted Beef
- 2 Tbsp Worchestershire
- 1/2 tsp black pepper
- 1 Tbsp Montreal steak seasoning
- 1 Tbsp minced garlic
- 2 Cups Milk
- 2 Tbsp Butter
- 2 Tbsp Flour
- 4 oz Provolone Cheese
- 8 oz American Cheese
- 8 oz Cheesewhiz

INSTRUCTIONS

Cut steak into bite size chunks and saute in a skillet with diced onion (Sprinkle just a little salt, pepper, and Montreal steak seasoning). Add to soup pot. Saute bell pepper in skillet and then add to soup pot. Add broth, consomme, Better Than Bouillon, Worcestershire, pepper, Montreal steak seasoning, and garlic. Cook until it boils and let simmer for 20 minutes.

While simmering, melt butter in a pan and whisk in flour until it is a thick paste. Stir in milk and bring to a boil. Add shredded or small sliced provolone a little at a time and whisk until melted into a sauce.

At the end of the simmering period, stir in provolone sauce***. Slice American cheese in small pieces and add to soup. Add cheesewhiz. Stir, turn heat to medium to bring back to boil. Let simmer and serve in a bowl with a bread roll on the side.

Directions Cont.

***Provolone Cheese Sauce

We used a recipe we found at https://www.realmomkitchen.com/wprm_print/provolone-cheese-sauce-for-cheesesteaks.

1 Tbsp butter
1 ½ Tbsp flour
1 cup milk
¼ cup or 2 oz grated Provolone cheese
Salt and Pepper to taste

In a sauce pan, melt butter and whisk in flour. Cook for a minute or two until the mixture turns a light brown. Slowly whisk in milk and bring to a boil. Remove from heat and add in the cheese.
Whisk together until the cheese is melted. Season with salt and pepper to taste.

History & Inspiration

The food Philadelphia is known for is the philly cheesesteak sandwich, which originated in 1930 when a hot dog vendor decided to do something different, changing out the hot dog for chopped beef with cooked onions. Around a decade later, cheese entered the picture. The three cheeses a patron may choose from at different cheesesteak establishments are provolone, cheez whiz, and American. Since several food vendors in Philadelphia already have the best cheesesteaks, we decided to create a philly cheesesteak soup.

NEW YORK

THE FOUR "BELLS" OF LIFE CIDER

> "Keeping time, time, time,
> In a sort of Runic rhyme,
> To the throbbing of the bells —
> Of the bells, bells, bells —"
>
> *The Bells - 1849*

INGREDIENTS

- 10 oz. Apple Cider
- 2 oz. Dr. Byrd or Jamaican Rum
- 1 Cinnamon Stick
- 1/2 oz. Falernum
- 1/2 oz. Allspice Dram
- 1/2 Barspoon Tiki Bitters

INSTRUCTIONS

Heat up the cider with a cinnamon stick in it. Stir in the rest of the ingredients to the heated cider and enjoy.

Inspiration

As mentioned in the Pepper Bells recipe, the bells: silver bells, golden bells, brazen bells, and iron bells are very reminiscent of the stages from birth to death. In creating this cider, Jeff matched up one ingredient to each bell. The apple cider represents the silver bells, thinking of how youth drink apple juice in their formative years. The rum represents the golden bells, a time settling into the comforts of adulthood. The falernum represents the brazen or alarum bells with its funky flavor, feeling bold in the autumn of life. The allspice dram represents the iron bells with its solid flavor to warm in the winter of life.

NEW YORK

LANDOR'S COTTAGE COOKIES

> "In fact, nothing could well be more simple — more utterly unpretending than this cottage. Its marvellous effect lay altogether in its artistic arrangement as a picture."
>
> *Landor's Cottage - 1849*

INGREDIENTS

- 2 ¾ Cups All Purpose Flour
- ½ tsp Salt
- ½ Cup Butter, softened
- 1 Cup Sugar
- 2 ¾ tsp Baking Powder
- 3 Eggs, well beaten
- ½ Cup Half and Half
- 1 tsp Vanilla Extract
- 1 tsp Cinnamon
- 1 Cup of Apples, peeled and chopped in small pieces

INSTRUCTIONS

Mix dry ingredients together and set aside. Mix butter and eggs together. Add butter and egg mixture and vanilla to dry ingredients. Mix in apples last. Place spoonfuls onto a cookie sheet. Bake at 400 degrees for 10-16 minutes or until golden brown. Ovens vary, so if your oven cooks quickly, lower your time. These cookies will be crunchy on the outside, but cakelike on the inside. Enjoy!

Inspiration

Poe lived in more than one location in New York, but the last place he lived in his life was in Fordham, this house is now known as the Bronx Cottage. Poe, Virginia, and Maria Clemm moved to this cottage because in Poe's time, it was out in the country on farmland, which would be good for Virginia's condition, tuberculosis. In *Landor's Cottage*, he references elements of this cottage and the surrounding area in his writing. Since apples are a largely produced fruit in New York, we felt like an apple cookie would bring about the country life in Fordham, NY while Poe lived there.

NEW YORK

RATIOCINATION APPLE PIE

> "I now remembered that in fact a fruiterer, carrying upon his head a large basket of apples..."
>
> *Murders in the Rue Morgue - 1841*

INGREDIENTS

6 Apples, different varieties
1/2 Cup Sugar
1/2 Cup Demerara Sugar
1 1/2 tsp Cinnamon
1/4 tsp Nutmeg
1/4 tsp Allspice
2 Tbsp Flour
2 Tbsp Butter, place on top of apple mixture before covering.

INSTRUCTIONS

Peel and slice your apples in thin slices. Add apples, white sugar, and Demerara sugar, cinnamon, nutmeg, allspice, and flour into a large mixing bowl, making sure to coat the apples thoroughly with the spices, flour, and sugar. Use either a pre-made pie crust or make your own. One we like to use is found at https://sallysbakingaddiction.com/baking-basics-homemade-buttery-flaky-pie-crust/.

Brush top of pie with milk or half and half, just a thin layer. Sprinkle sugar on top. Bake 25 minutes on 375 with edges wrapped with foil. Remove foil and bake 20-25 more minutes.

History & Inspiration

New York state is the 2nd largest producer of apples with Washington state coming in first. Therefore, we had to include Carmen's homemade apple pie she always makes at Thanksgiving and in the fall when the local orchard near her home has apples in season. Since ratiocination means logical reasoning, we felt the title should include the word since Poe's detective, C. Auguste Dupin, uses this type of thinking to solve mysteries. The key to giving this pie such flavor is to use six different styles of apples, some sweet and some tart.

RECIPE FOR DISASTER: ONE TROUBLED POET, ONE BEAUTIFUL WIDOW, AND ONE UNFORGIVING CITY— EDGAR ALLAN POE IN PROVIDENCE, RHODE ISLAND

It was a sultry July evening in 1845 when Edgar Allan Poe first visited Providence. He was invited by his friend, Frances Osgood, to attend a literary lecture that she was giving downtown. After the lecture, Poe and Osgood took a late-night walk through the east side of the city. While travelling north on Benefit Street, Poe caught a glimpse of an ethereal-looking woman tending a rose garden in the backyard of her home. Osgood happened to know this enigmatic figure, and that's when Poe first learned of Sarah Helen Whitman, a widowed poetess native to Providence. Clad in a white muslin dress, a sheer veil, and a white shawl, Whitman's garments were illuminated by a full moon as they floated in the warm, evening breeze. This scene left an indelible mark in Poe's mind, prompting him to write a poem about the occurrence three years later. The poem was his second titled "To Helen," and was sent anonymously to Whitman in response to an unsolicited Valentine poem that she had written for him. This exchange of flirtatious poetry ignited a courtship that would take place from September until December, 1848.

Photo: Whitman's Backyard Circa 2024

THE WORDS OF LEVI LIONEL LELAND

After rejecting Poe's proposal of marriage on their first date, Whitman eventually agreed to a conditional engagement about a month later, asking Poe to abstain from alcohol in order to marry her. Poe vowed sobriety and the couple planned to marry on Christmas. On December 23, just two days before the wedding, Poe and Whitman were visiting their favorite library, The Providence Athenaeum, when Whitman was passed an anonymous note informing her that Poe was seen drinking at his hotel. No longer able to bear Poe's perilous behavior, Whitman called off the wedding. They never spoke again and Poe died less than a year later in Baltimore, Maryland.

Despite the circumstances surrounding their breakup, Whitman was devastated by the news of Poe's death. She composed a number of poems lamenting him and their romance together. Whitman also became one of Poe's most staunch defenders against the slanders that were being published about him by his literary rival, Rufus Griswold. In 1860, Whitman used her platform as an accomplished poetess and essayist to publish her own biography of Poe titled Edgar Poe and His Critics. She went on to correspond with Poe's earliest biographers to ensure that the most accurate information be published about Poe for the world to read. The alluring city of Providence witnessed Poe during one of the most fascinating and final years of his life, while producing one of the most significant players in his legacy, Sarah Helen Whitman. For that, let's raise a glass of coffee milk to Edgar Allan Poe, Sarah Helen Whitman, and Providence, Rhode Island!

For more information about Edgar Allan Poe's time in Providence, Sarah Helen Whitman, and their tempestuous romance, visit www.edgarallanpoeri.com.

PROVIDENCE

COFFEE MILK COCKTAIL

> "It was his practice to take a very large dose of it immediately after breakfast, each morning — or rather immediately after a cup of strong coffee..."
>
> *A Tale of the Ragged Mountains - 1844*

INGREDIENTS

- 2 ounces of brandy
- 4 ounces of milk
- 1 ounce of Autocrat coffee syrup (plus a little extra for drizzle)
- Coffee beans for garnish

INSTRUCTIONS

Shake all ingredients together with ice until cold and frothy. Pour over a glass filled with fresh ice and lightly drizzle more coffee syrup on top. Garnish with coffee beans and enjoy!

History

John Bartlett was born in Providence and served as Secretary of State for Rhode Island between 1855 and 1872. He was one of the original founders of The Providence Athenaeum, a library in which Poe and Whitman frequented during their courtship. In 1836, Bartlett moved to New York and opened a bookstore that Poe often visited and browsed. During this time, the two men became good friends. In one recollection, Bartlett recalled that he had "never seen [Poe] inspired by any more dangerous stimulant than strong coffee, of which he was very fond of and of which he drank freely." It is also documented that Whitman would often prepare Poe a cup of coffee during his visits to her home.

Inspiration

Given this testimony of Poe's love for coffee, he would undoubtedly enjoy this cocktail utilizing Rhode Island's official state drink, coffee milk! For a Sarah Helen Whitman-approved version of this drink, hold the brandy...

LIL' RHODY ROCKS

> "He talked on, therefore, at great length, while I merely leaned back in my chair with my eyes shut, and amused myself with munching raisins and fillipping the stems about the room."
>
> *The Angel of the Odd - 1844*

INGREDIENTS

- 1 pound of white candy coating or meltng chips, chopped
- ½ cup of milk chocolate chips
- 1 cup of semisweet chocolate chips
- 1 cup of mini pretzels, slightly broken
- 1 cup of raisins
- 1 cup of dry roasted, salted peanuts

INSTRUCTIONS

In a saucepan, cook candy coating and chocolate chips over low heat, stirring frequently until melted and smooth. Let that cool for about 10 minutes before stirring in the pretzels, raisins, and peanuts.

Line a baking sheet with parchment or waxed paper and drop rounded tablespoonfuls of the mixture onto it, leaving space between each cluster. Refrigerate for about 45 minutes or until candy is firm. Enjoy!

History

Sarah Helen Whitman had many friends and admirers who wrote various recollections of her after her death. One of these friends was a man named William Bailey, a professor of botany at Brown University. He wrote, "Mrs. Whitman had an inordinate love of candy, some days I think existed upon it alone."

Inspiration

This is an old Rhode Island family recipe combining peanuts, pretzels, and raisins, with rich, creamy chocolate. These sweet and salty candy clusters would certainly satisfy Whitman's sweet tooth!

BALTIMORE

THE COOPER'S DOWNFALL

> "I am very anxious to remain and settle myself in Balto [Baltimore] as Mr. Allan has married again and I no longer look upon Richmond as my place of residence..."
>
> *Edgar writes to William Gwynn, owner of the Baltimore Gazette and Daily Advertiser - May 6, 1831*

INGREDIENTS

1 ounce Sagamore Spirits Rye

1/2 ounce creme de peche

1 large fresh pineapple chunk

3/4 ounce lime juice, freshly squeezed

1 ounce honey syrup

½ tsp Old Bay

8 large mint leaves

¾ Cup Ice

Garnish: mint leaf

INSTRUCTIONS

In a blender, add all ingredients, including ice. Blend for about 20 seconds until mixture is smooth and slushy. Pour mixture into a coupe glass or tiki mug and garnish with a mint leaf and/or pineapple chunk.

History

While Poe lived in Baltimore, MD for a short time, he revisited the city several times over his lifetime. He was in Baltimore in 1827 before he enlisted in the army. From 1829-30, he visited his brother, William Leonard Henry Poe, and Maria Clemm's family. In 1831, he moved back to Baltimore after he left West Point, where he stayed until 1835 before moving back to Richmond, VA. Poe visited Baltimore many times between 1835 and 1849.

On October 3, 1849, election day, Poe was found near Gunner's Hall, a polling place. He was disheveled, delirious, wearing clothes that did not belong to him. He was taken to Washington Hospital, where he died on October 7, 1849.

Inspiration

Based on the days prior to October 3rd, the details of how Poe was found, and the symptoms he had, there are many theories around the mystery of how Poe actually died. One theory is the practice of cooping. Cooping is where people would often kidnap voters at polling places, force them to drink lots of alcohol, sometimes beating them, and changing their clothes and appearance repeatedly so the voter could continuously vote, acting as different people. This is where the inspiration for this cocktail derived from in addition to the drink being a riff on the tiki cocktail, The Missionary's Downfall, which contains white rum, peach liqueur or brandy, honey syrup, fresh pineapple chunks or juice, fresh lime juice, and mint leaves. To create the Cooper's Downfall, we changed the rum for Sagamore Spirits Rye, which is distilled in Baltimore, and we added Old Bay seasoning.

THINGUM BOB'S MARYLAND STYLE CRAB CAKES

> "Here Mr. Crab concluded, and the tears stood in his eyes."
>
> *The Literary Life of Thingum Bob, Esq - 1844*

INGREDIENTS

- 1 lb Crab meat, preferably jumbo lump
- 1/2 Cup Sour Cream
- 1 Tbsp Olive Oil
- 1 Tsp Lemon Juice
- 1 Tbsp Old Bay Seasoning
- 1 sleeve Buttery Crackers, crushed
- 1/2 Cup Bread Crumbs
- 1 Tsp Worcestershire Sauce
- 1 Tbsp Parsley
- 1 Green Onions
- 1 Tbsp Frank's Hot Sauce
- 1 Tbsp Dijon Mustard
- 1 Egg
- 1/3 Cup Mayonnaise

INSTRUCTIONS

Mix all ingredients together, except olive oil, and shape into 2"-3" patties. Place olive oil in a frying pan, flip the patties a few times, frying approximately 3-5 minutes (if patties are thicker, it will take a few minutes longer) and cooking until golden brown on the outside. To ensure the patties are cooked thoroughly, checking the internal temperature with a cooking thermometer will be at 165 degrees Fahrenheit.

REMOULADE SAUCE

INGREDIENTS

1 cup mayonnaise
1 tablespoon dijon mustard
1 tablespoon ketchup
1 Tbsp garlic minced
2 teaspoons fresh horseradish or prepared horseradish
1 teaspoon lemon juice ideally fresh
2 Tbsp parsley
1 green onion (scallion) finely chopped
1 tsp Old Bay
1 teaspoon Paprika
2 teaspoons Frank's Hot Sauce

INSTRUCTIONS

Mix all ingredients together and let sit in the refrigerator for a few hours before serving over warm Maryland Style Crab Cakes.

History & Inspiration

Maryland style crab cakes are a staple in the Baltimore area. What sets apart Maryland style is the jumbo lump crab meat used. The cakes are also pan fried. Questions are raised as to where did the crab cakes originate with no definitive answer. However, frying dates back to the 1630s, so crab cake recipes from the Chesapeake Bay region are historical in a culinary sense.

A TALE OF THE OLD BAY CHEDDAR CHEESE RISOTTO

> "Beyond the limits of the city arose, in frequent majestic groups, the palm and the cocoa, with other gigantic and wierd [[weird]] trees of vast age; and here and there might be seen a field of rice, the thatched hut of a peasant, a tank, a stray temple, a gypsy camp, or a solitary graceful maiden taking her way, with a pitcher upon her head, to the banks of the magnificent river."

A Tale of the Ragged Mountains - 1844

INGREDIENTS

- 3 cups beef broth
- 2 tbsp olive oil
- 1 tsp dried onion flakes
- 1 tbsp minced garlic
- 1 cup of arborio rice
- 1/4 cup white wine
- 4 tbsp butter
- 3/4 cup shredded cheddar cheese
- 2 tsp Old Bay

INSTRUCTIONS

In an instant-pot, turn on saute function. Add the olive oil, garlic, and onion flakes. Cook until oil starts heating up and bubbles. Add the rice, stir until coated. Continue to stir and cook rice until it is toasted. If you stop stirring, it will stick to the bottom. Pour in white wine and continue to stir for about 30 seconds. Turn off the instant-pot. Add the beef broth and old bay. Stir to combine. Close and lock the lid. Select high pressure according to manufacture's instructions. Set the timer for 6 minutes. Start the instant-pot.

Once the instant-pot is done, release the pressure according to the manufactures release method. After 5 minutes, unlock and remove the lid. Add butter and stir until melted and risotto is creamy. Stir in cheddar cheese until melted.

History & Inspiration

Old Bay seasoning has been around since 1940 thanks to Gustav Brunn. He started the Baltimore Spice Company in 1930. Crab steamers would blend spices they bought from his shop for their crabs and Brunn was inspired by them to create his own crab seasoning; thus, the birth of Old Bay.

Jeff and Carmen love Old Bay seasoning and they love risotto. So, they felt like a risotto with Old Bay would taste splendid. They had never had a risotto made with cheddar cheese, thinking Old Bay would pair well with the seasoning. They tried it and loved it. They felt this was a great pairing of flavors to pay homage to one of Poe's places so important to his legacy.

CHAPTER

SEVEN

VIVIDLY BLUE CRAB DIP

"That at the eastern extremity was hung, for example, in blue — and vividly blue were its windows."

"The Masque of the Red Death" - 1842

INGREDIENTS

1 Tbsp Olive oil

1/4 tsp salt

1/8 tsp White pepper

1/2 tsp paprika

1 Tbsp chopped onion

2 tsp Garlic powder

2 tbsp Old Bay

3/4 lb white American cheese, cubed

1 lb blue crab meat

INSTRUCTIONS

In a medium skillet, add the olive oil on medium heat. Add the crab meat, onion, and all of the spices. Cook until the onions become translucent. Turn the heat down and add the cheese. Keep stirring the mixture until the cheese is melted throughout the dip. Serve warm with blue corn tortilla chips.

INSPIRATION

140

For the appetizer as the first course for the Masque of the Red Death feast, we thought a crab dip would be a fantastic way to begin. Crab is prevalent in the Northeast, especially Maryland. So, we thought it fitting to introduce this dip.

PRINCE PROSPERO'S PURPLE STEW

> "The second chamber was purple in its ornaments and tapestries, and here the panes were purple."
>
> *"The Masque of the Red Death" - 1842*

INGREDIENTS

- 1 lb beef stew meat
- 2 Tbsp minced garlic
- 3 Tbsp flour
- 1/5 head of purple cabbage
- 1 Radicchio
- 1 Cup and a half of purple carrots
- 1/2 purple onion
- 1 Cup and a half of purple potatoes
- 3 Heirloom tomatoes
- 2 tsp Old Bay
- 1 tsp Salt
- 1 tsp coarse black pepper
- 1/2 tsp Oregano
- 1 tsp dried Rosemary
- 1 tsp Parsley
- 1 tsp Basil
- Beef broth, pour until reaching the top of the mixture

INSPIRATION

The Purple room came second, and so for a seven course meal, a soup was our choice for the second course. Even though there will only be a hint of some purple elements after the stew is cooked, most of the ingredients going in are purple.

INSTRUCTIONS

Cut up the cabbage, raddichio, carrots onion, potatoes, and tomatoes. Place stew meat in bottom of a crockpot, add all spices on top of the meat, layering vegetables starting with the onions. Add the flour to a half cup of the beef broth, mixing it until flour dissolves. Pour that into the crockpot. After all ingredients are in the crockpot, pour beef broth until everything is covered. Cook on low for 7-8 hours and stew meat is tender.

SAGACIOUS SALAD

> "The third was green throughout, and so were the casements."
>
> *"The Masque of the Red Death"* - 1842

INGREDIENTS

Green leaf lettuce

4 Cucumbers

2 Granny Smith Apples

2 Green bell pepper

1 cup Pistachios

Tomatillo Dressing

1/4 Cup Olive Oil

1/3 Cup Tomatillo Salsa

1 tsp Tajin seasoning

1/4 tsp Garlic Powder

1/2 tsp Honey

1 tsp Cilantro

INSTRUCTIONS

For the salad, slice cucumbers, apples, and bell peppers after washing. Wash and cut lettuce in smaller pieces. Place the lettuce on a plate.

For dressing, slightly warm the honey for 10 seconds in the microwave. Place all ingredients in a cruet/container that seals to shake the dressing until it is mixed completely.

Add the dressing to the mixture of cucumbers, apples, peppers, and pistachios. Pour mixture over the lettuce and serve.

INSPIRATION

For the Green room, and the third course, a salad was the perfect selection. With this salad, you may keep to the recipe, or add some variety and creativity with adding different spices or flavored oils and or vinegars.

ROSEMARY PORK A LA ORANGE

> "The fourth was furnished and litten with orange"
>
> *"The Masque of the Red Death" - 1842*

INGREDIENTS

- 3-4 lb. Pork loin
- Small bag Medley New Potatoes*
- ½ Onion Diced
- Small bag Baby Carrots
- 2 Honeycrisp Apples Sliced
- 1 tsp. Salt
- 1 tsp. White Pepper
- 1 tsp. Garlic Powder
- 1 tsp. Ground Rosemary
- 1 Jar Orange Marmalade
- 2 Cans Ginger Ale

INSTRUCTIONS

Pat meat with salt, pepper, garlic powder, and rosemary and place meat at bottom of the crockpot. Add the cut apples around the pork loin. Add the onion, carrots, and potatoes next. Cover the meat, apples, and vegetables with the marmalade. Pour the 2 cans of ginger ale over the top. Cover the crockpot and cook on low for around 8 hours or until the pork loin shreds easily.

*If you are creating the entire feast with the Garlic Mashed Potatoes, eliminate new potatoes from this recipe.

INSPIRATION

The fourth room Prince Prospero enters in Poe's story, *The Masque of the Red Death*, is the Orange room. We felt this entree was befitting a prince with its regal name and sweet and sour flavors for the pallet.

GHASTLY GARLIC MASHED POTATOES

> "the fifth with white"
>
> *"The Masque of the Red Death" - 1842*

INGREDIENTS

2 cups Peeled Red Potatoes Diced

3 cups Water

2 tsp. Salt (½ tsp. Cooking potatoes; 1 ½ tsp. finishing potatoes after draining water)

1 Cup Heavy Cream

4 Cloves Garlic

½ tsp. White Pepper

2 Tbsp Unsalted Butter

INSTRUCTIONS

In a medium saucepan, combine the potatoes, water, and ½ tsp. salt bringing to a boil over high heat. Reduce the heat to medium-high and cook until tender for around 8-10 minutes. Remove from the heat and drain in a colander.

Place the potatoes back in the pot over medium heat, add the heavy cream, garlic, and remaining 1 ½ tsp. salt, and white pepper. Mash vigorously with a potato masher until fairly smooth removing all lumps. Whisk in butter and remove from heat. Serve Immediately.

INSPIRATION

The White room is the fourth room Prince Prospero went through during *The Masque of the Red Death*. To celebrate the White room for the feast, we added this recipe as a side to accompany the Rosemary Pork a la Orange if you choose not to add potatoes to the pork roast.

THREE SUNDAES IN A WEEK WITH RUMGUDGEON SAUCE

"the sixth with violet"
"The Masque of the Red Death" - 1842

"I say, you shall have Kate and her plum when three Sundays come together in a week — but not till then — you young scapegrace — not till then, if I die for it."

Three Sundays in a Week - 1841

INGREDIENTS

1/4 cup water

1/4 cup plum jam

2 Tbsp butter

1/4 cup Dr. Byrd Rum

1/2 cup Demerara sugar

Chocolate Ice Cream

Vanilla Ice Cream

Coffee Ice Cream

Plum wedge and blueberries for garnish

INSTRUCTIONS

For the Rumgudgeon sauce, melt butter in a sauce pan over medium heat. Once melted, whisk in plum jam until smooth. Add water and Dr. Byrd rum and whisk until blended. Whisk in sugar. Bring to low boil and reduce heat to Med/Low and simmer until a syrup consistency. Whisk periodically. Remove from heat, pour into a small measuring pitcher (1-2 cups), and let cool down. Once cool, serve over one scoop of each: chocolate ice cream, vanilla ice cream, and coffee ice cream for each individual.

INSPIRATION

Three Sundays in a Week is one of Poe's more humorous stories. Uncle Rumgudgeon will not allow Bobby to marry his daughter, Kate, until three Sundays converge into one week. For the inspiration for this recipe, we felt like a play on words changing Sunday to Sundae, creating a delightful dessert. The three flavors of ice cream all complement each other, and so, we created a sauce based on plums since plums were mentioned in the story. Another element we used was the rum for Uncle Rumgudgeon for the sauce; therefore, the sauce is called Rumgudgeon Sauce to pour over the Three Sundaes in a Week. This may be garnished with a dollop of whipped cream, a slice of plum, and blueberries.

PROSPERO'S DEMISE

> "The seventh apartment was closely shrouded in black velvet tapestries that hung all over the ceiling and down the walls, falling in heavy folds upon a carpet of the same material and hue."

"The Masque of the Red Death" - 1842

INGREDIENTS

1 oz. Bourbon

½ oz. Mr. Black Coffee Liqueur

¾ Mozart Chocolate Dark Liqueur

½ Rich Simple Syrup

½ Bar spoon Fee Brother's Black Walnut Bitters

INSTRUCTIONS

Add ingredients over ice in a shaker and shake until the tin is ice cold. Strain the cocktail in a glass.

INSPIRATION

The Black Room-the seventh and final room- is where Prospero meets the Red Death and dies. The after dinner dessert cocktail is bittersweet, but delectable just as the uninvited guest to the masquerade brought down Prospero after he ran cowardly through all of the rooms to meet his demise in the Black room with the Ebony clock's pendulum swinging as the tolls of the bells struck midnight.

"And now was acknowledged the presence of the Red Death. He had come like a thief in the night. And one by one dropped the revellers in the blood-bedewed halls of their revel, and died each in the despairing posture of his fall. And the life of the ebony clock went out with that of the last of the gay. And the flames of the tripods expired. And Darkness and Decay and the Red Death held illimitable dominion over all."

THE FALL OF THE FLAVORED RAVEN

"While I gazed, this fissure rapidly widened — there came a fierce breath of the whirlwind — the entire orb of the satellite burst at once upon my sight — my brain reeled as I saw the mighty walls rushing asunder — there was a long tumultuous shouting sound like the voice of a thousand waters — and the deep and dank tarn at my feet closed sullenly and silently over the fragments of the "House of Usher."

The Fall of the House of Usher - 1839

1 oz. Despair
1 oz. Gloom
2 oz. Madness
1 oz. Destruction
½ oz. Delusion
1 Barspoon of Wormwood Bitters

"My flavors have fallen into the tarn. I can flavor...Nevermore!"

INSPIRATION

For *The Fall of the House of Usher*, we talked about creating a recipe for this story multiple times with no viable option. Why? Everything in the story is dark, dreary, and doomed. There were no flavors, scents, or visuals that were aesthetically pleasing to the palette; thus, we have the only drink befitting the flavors of the downtrodden house: Malort. This highly bitter alcohol is made from neutral spirits, wormwood, and sugar. Basically, this would be like drinking from the tarn.

Photo credited to Beau Vincent, A Breezetonian

APPENDIX

A Dream Within a Dream..81, 87

A Predicament...117

A Tale of the Ragged Mountains..127, 135

A Thousand-and-Second Tale of Scheherazade..................................51

Annabel Lee...3, 25, 41

Diddling as Considered One of the Exact Sciences............................17

Dream-Land..6, 91

Eldorado...85

Eulalie..6

Eureka..57

Four Beasts in One..11

Hop-Frog..65

King Pest..9

Landor's Cottage..121

Lionizing..95

Mellonta Tauta..59

Never Bet the Devil Your Head..75

Politian...19

Serenade..103

The Angel of the Odd..97, 129

The Balloon Hoax..53

The Bells..21, 119

The Black Cat..39

The Cask of Amontillado	35, 37, 63, 73
The Devil in the Belfry	71
The Fall of the House of Usher	153
The Gold-Bug	47, 49, 111
The Island of the Fay	83
The Journal of Julius Rodman	113
The Literary Life of Thingum Bob	133
The Man of the Crowd	107
The Man that was Used Up	105
The Masque of the Red Death	139-152
The Murders in the Rue Morgue	15, 33, 123
The Narrative of Arthur Gordon Pym of Nantucket	93
The Oblong Box	77
The Pit and the Pendulum	69
The Purloined Letter	23
The Raven	7, 29
The Sleeper	89
The System of Dr. Tarr and Professor Fether	13
The Tell-Tale Heart	31, 67
The Unparalled Journey of One Hans Pfall	55
The Valley of Unrest	5, 6
Three Sundays in a Week	149
To One in Paradise	6

Simple syrup is made by heating water and mixing in the sugar until it completely dissolves. This allows the sugars to mix into the cold drinks where adding straight sugar would not mix and sink to the bottom.

Most simple sugar is made as a 1 to 1 mixture. This means 10 ounces of sugar and 10 ounces of water.

A rich simple syrup is made as a 2 to 1 mixture. This would mean 10 ounces of sugar to 5 ounces of water.

From researching drink history it appears the rich simple syrup was how it was made in the 1800s. 1 reason is it adds the sweetness without adding much water. The other reason is that it is shelf stable. It cannot mold due to the low water content. Thus it can sit unrefrigerated for months. It will most likely crystalize if you don't use it, but it will not go bad.

Regular simple syrup is made with standard white sugar. Demerara sugar is a minimally processed sugar that still has a high amount of molasses and larger grains. This makes the syrup a bit less sweet and has a richer flavor with hints of caramel and toffee. I had to order it online. In stores I was able to find Turbinado sugar which is a bit more refined than Demerara but not as refined as granulated sugar.

If you have a 1:1 simple syrup for your recipes you may want to up the amount slightly to increase the sugar in the recipe.

INDEX

A

Allspice Dram: 31, 49, 119
Allspice, Ground: 109, 123
Amaro Montenegro: 63
Amontillado: 29, 63, 73
Ancho Reyes Chile Liqueur: 37, 65
Apple: 121, 123
Apple, Granny Smith: 143
Apple, Honeycrisp: 145
Apple Cider: 9, 119
Asian Seasoning: 41
Asparagus: 73
Autocrat Coffee Syrup: 127

B

Bacon: 13, 43
Bacon Drippings: 43
Baking Powder: 55, 93, 109, 121
Baking Soda: 43
Basil, Dried: 73, 141
Beef Broth: 15, 117, 135, 141
Beef Consommé: 117
Beef, Ground: 15, 21
Beef, Stew Meat: 141
Beer: 89
Better Than Bullion Roasted Beef: 117
BG Reynolds Paradise Blend: 65
Bitters, Allspice: 85
Bitters, Angostura: 63, 107
Bitters, Bitterman's Burlesque: 85
Bitters, Bitterman's Tiki: 31, 83, 119
Bitters, Fee Brother's Aztec Chocolate: 63, 67, 91
Bitters, Fee Brother's Black Walnut: 33, 35, 151
Bitters, Old Forrester Smoked Cinnamon: 37
Bitters, Smoked Chili: 7
Blueberry: 149
Blackberry: 33
Blue Curacao: 29
Bourbon: 151
Bourbon, Angel's Envy: 29
Bourbon, Evan Williams BiB: 105
Bourbon, Four Roses Small Batch: 35
Brandy: 127
Bread Crumbs: 133
Butter: 15, 19, 25, 26, 43, 44, 53, 57, 73, 77, 87, 89, 91, 93, 95, 97, 109, 117, 121, 123, 135, 147, 149
Butterscotch Schnapps: 29

C

Cabbage, Purple: 141
Cake Mix, White: 97
Caramel: 25
Carrots, Baby: 145
Carrots, Purple: 141
Cayenne Pepper: 41
Champagne: 67
Cheese, American: 117
Cheese, Cheddar: 15, 87, 135
Cheese, Provolone: 117
Cheese, Variety: 69
Cheese, White American: 139
Cheesewhiz: 117
Cherry, Maraschino: 67

Chicken: 13, 73, 75
Chicken Broth: 13, 95
Chili Powder: 95
Chives, Dried: 87, 91
Chocolate Chips, Milk: 129
Chocolate Chips, Semisweet: 129
Chocolate Kiss: 81
Chocolate, White Melting: 129
Cilantro: 143
Cinnamon Stick: 119
Cinnamon, Ground: 53, 109, 121, 123
Cinnamon/Nutmeg Spice Mix: 65
Clemant Creole Schrubb: 49
Cloves, Ground: 105
Cocoa Powder: 25, 44
Coconut Flavorings: 97
Coconut, Sweet Flakes: 97
Coffee Beans: 127
Cognac: 7, 35
Cooking Sherry: 73
Corn: 13
Cornstarch: 13, 57, 59
Crab: 133
Crab, Blue: 139
Crackers, Buttery: 133
Cream Cheese: 26, 39, 58
Creme de Peche: 131
Creme de Violette: 5
Crescent Rolls: 11
Crown Royale Vanilla: 101
Cucumbers: 17, 143
Cumin, Ground: 95

D

Dressing, Sundried Tomato: 23

E

Eggs: 21, 25, 43, 55, 57, 71, 77, 97, 121, 133
Elderberry Liqueur: 5

F

Falernum: 83, 119
Fish, Red Snapper: 41
Flour, All Purpose: 15, 25, 43, 55, 73, 87, 93, 95, 109, 121
Flour, General: 77, 117, 123, 141
Flour, Self-Rising: 89
Food Coloring, Black Gel: 25
Food Coloring, Green: 78
Food Coloring, Your Choice: 26
Franks Hot Sauce: 133, 134
Frosting, Vanilla Buttercream: 97

G

Garlic, Minced: 13, 15, 41, 73, 91, 111, 117, 134, 135, 141, 147
Garlic, Powder: 17, 19, 23, 39, 75, 87, 89, 139, 143, 145
Gin, Floral: 5
Gin, London Dry: 103, 107, 113
Ginger, Ground: 105, 111
Ginger, Minced: 19
Ginger Ale: 145
Graham Crackers, Honey: 57
Grape Juice: 65

H

Half and Half: 13, 73, 81, 121
Ham: 105
Heavy Cream: 44, 147
Honey: 9, 78, 143
Honey Syrup: 131
Horseradish: 134

I

Ice: 131
Ice Cream, Chocolate: 149
Ice Cream, Coffee: 149
Ice Cream, Vanilla: 149
Irish Cream: 101
Italian Seasoning: 75

J

Jam, Plum: 149

K

Ketchup: 134

L

Lemon: 3, 9, 29, 49, 55, 56, 65, 77, 83, 91, 113, 133, 134
Lemon Zest: 55, 77
Lettuce, Green Leaf: 143
Lettuce, Romaine: 23
Liquor: 43 37
Lime: 3, 31, 51, 131
Lime, Key: 111
Limoncello: 97
Lobster: 91

M

Malort: 153
Maple Syrup: 43, 44, 115
Maraschino Liqueur: 103
Mayonnaise: 133, 134
Melon Liqueur: 3
Mexcal Blanco: 7, 29
Milk: 15, 43, 55, 57, 87, 93, 109, 117, 127
Milk, Butter: 25, 77, 78
Mint Leaves: 115, 131
Miracle Whip: 71
Montreal Steak Seasoning: 15, 117
Moonshine: 3, 5
Mozart Chocolate Dark: 101, 151
Mr. Black: 7, 33, 151
Mustard: 71
Mustard, Dijon: 105, 133, 134
Mustard, Ground: 13

N

Nutmeg, Ground: 53, 77, 109, 123

O

Oil, Cooking: 55
Oil, Italian Lemon Olive: 41
Oil, Olive: 17, 19, 73, 75, 133, 135, 139, 143
Oil, Vegetable: 25
Old Bay: 13, 47, 131, 133, 134, 135, 139, 141
Olive: 69
Olive, Black: 75
Onion: 13, 15, 21, 73, 75, 111, 117, 139, 145
Onion Powder: 39
Onion, Dried Flakes: 135
Onion, Green: 133, 134
Onion, Purple: 141

Orange Extract: 57
Orange Liqueur: 47, 51, 57, 81
Orange Marmalade: 145
Oranges, Mandarin: 58, 83
Oregano, Dried: 13, 73, 141
Orgeat: 65

P

Paprika: 41, 71, 75, 134, 139
Paprika, Spanish: 93
Parsley, Dried: 73, 133, 134, 141
Pasta: 75
Peaches: 109, 111
Peanuts, Dry-Roasted-Salted: 129
Pepper, Black: 15, 17, 19, 21, 23, 71, 117, 141
Pepper, Jalapeno: 39
Pepper, White: 13, 39, 73, 75, 91, 95, 139, 145, 147
Pepperoni: 11
Peppers, Bell: 13, 21, 39, 117, 143
Peppers, Sweet: 17, 39, 73, 75, 111
Pickles, Spicey Maple Bourbon: 71
Pineapple Juice: 23
Pineapple, Crushed: 23
Pineapple, Fresh: 23, 131
Pistachios: 143
Plum: 113, 115, 149
Pomegranate Juice: 51
Poppy Seed: 55
Pork Loin Roast: 23, 145
Potatoes, Medley: 145
Potatoes, Purple: 141
Potatoes, Red: 13, 147
Potatoes, Russet: 15
Potatoes, Sweet: 53
Pretzel Sticks: 69
Pretzels Mioni: 129
Prosciutto: 11
Prosecco: 67

R

Radicchio: 141
Raisin: 129
Ranch Season Mix: 39
Rhum Agricole: 37
Ribeye: 117
Rice: 21
Rice, Arborio: 135
Rosemary, Dried: 73, 89, 141
Rosemary, Ground: 145
Rum, Aged Dominican: 49
Rum, Demerara: 83, 85
Rum, Don Q Puerto Rican: 31
Rum, Dr. Bird: 149
Rum, Dr. Bird Pineapple: 31, 83
Rum, Jamaican: 119
Rum, Royal Jamaican Dark: 33
Rum, White: 47
Rye Whiskey: 107, 115, 131

S

Sage: 21
Salami: 11
Salsa, Tomatillo: 143
Salt: 13, 15, 17, 19, 21, 23, 39, 44, 55, 57, 71, 73, 75, 93, 109, 111, 121, 139, 141, 145, 147
Salt, Garlic: 87
Salt, Sea: 3, 5, 25, 31, 95
Shortening: 77, 87
Simple Syrup, Rich: 3, 31, 51, 113, 151
Simple Syrup, Rich Demerara: 33, 35, 47, 49, 85
Sour Cream: 39, 133
Soy Sauce: 41
Squash, Butternut: 19
Sausage, Cocktail: 11
Sausage, Ground Pork: 21
Sugar, Brown: 19, 53, 75, 109, 111
Sugar, Demerara: 93, 105, 109, 123, 149
Sugar, Powdered: 26, 44, 56, 78
Sugar, White: 25, 43, 55, 57, 59, 71, 77, 89, 109, 121, 123

T

Tajin: 93, 143
Tea, Green: 78
Tea, Peach: 49
Tennessee Whiskey: 9
Tequila: 51, 65
Teriyaki Sauce: 23
Thyme, Dried: 73
Tomato Soup: 21
Tomatoes, Cherry: 17, 73, 75, 111
Tomatoes, Diced: 15
Tomatoes, Heirloom: 141
Tortilla, Flour: 59

V

Vanilla Extract: 25, 26, 59, 77, 121
Vinegar: 25
Vinegar, Apple Cider: 105
Vinegar, Balsamic: 17, 75
Vinegar, Ginger Balsamic: 41
Vinegar, White Balsamic: 111

W

Walnuts: 57, 58
Water: 9, 23, 59, 93, 147, 149
Water, Carbonated: 113
Watermelon: 59
Whipped Topping: 58
White Chocolate Liqueur: 103
Wine, Chardonnay: 47
Wine, Merlot: 75
Wine, Tempranillo: 37
Wine, White: 135
Worcestershire Sauce: 117, 133

RESOURCES

A to E

American Songwriter: (**americansongwriter.com**)
- **The Meaning of the Weirdest Beatles Song, "I Am The Walrus"**, Catherine Walthall, July 9, 2022

Baltimore Heritage: (**explore.baltimoreheritage.org**)
- **Gustav Brunn's Baltimore Spice Company**, Francesca Cohen, October 25, 2022

Britannica Online Encyclopaedia: (**www.britannica.com**)
- **Salvador Dali**, *The Editors of Encyclopaedia Britannica*

Cape Porpoise Lobster Co.: (**www.capeporpoiselobster.com**)
- **Lobster and Chocolate: Unconventional Yet Perfect Pairings for Valentine's Day,** *Posted February 7, 2024 by Cape Porpoise Lobster*

Charleston County Public Library: (**www.ccpl.org**)
- **Edgar Allan Poe/Sullivan's Island Library**, 2025

Charleston Crab House: (**charlestoncrabhouse.com**)

Difford's Guide - For Discerning Drinkers: (**www.diffordsguide.com**)
- **Clover Club Cocktail**
- **History of Sour Cocktails**, Simon Difford

Edgar Allan Poe Society of Baltimore: (**www.eapoe.org**)
- Eugene L. Didier, "The Poe Cult," Bookman: A Magazine of Literature and Life, (New York, NY), December 1902, pp. 336-339
- The Poe Log: A Documentary Life of Edgar Allan Poe, 1809-1849 (1987)
- William C. Woolfson, "Flora Listings," Flora and Fauna in the Works of Edgar Allan Poe (1992), pp. 13-54
- Alexander Hammond, "A Reconstruction of Poe's 1833 Tales of the Folio Club, Preliminary Notes," from Poe Studies, vol. V, no. 2, December 1972, pp. 25-32
- Poe Studies, Volume V, Number 2 (December 1972)
- Edgar Allan Poe (ed. J. A. Harrison), "Three Sundays in a Week," The Complete Works of Edgar Allan Poe — Vol. IV: Tales - part 03 (1902), pg. 0229
- Edgar Allan Poe (ed. J. A. Harrison), "Marginalia - Part I," The Complete Works of Edgar Allan Poe — Vol. XVI: Marginalia and Eureka (1902), pg. 0007
- The Collected Writings of Edgar Allan Poe, EAP: Eureka (2004)
- Edgar Allan Poe (ed. T. O. Mabbott), "Four Beasts in One," The Collected Works of Edgar Allan Poe — Vol. II: Tales and Sketches (1978), pp. 117-130
- Edgar Allan Poe in Baltimore
- Poe's Memorial Grave

G to O

GetHandyOutdoors: (gethandyoutdoors.com)
- **Yes, You Can Grow Plums in Pennsylvania Here's How to Succeed**, Luke H., August, 6, 2024

House of Apple Jay: (www.houseofapplejay.com)
- The Origins of Rum Punch: **How the Caribbean's Boldest Spirit Conquered Colonial Punch Bowls**

*How Sweet * Eats*: (www.howsweeteats.com)
- Our Favorite Warm & Buttery Lobster Rolls!, Jessica, June 21, 2021.

imbibe - liquid culture: (imbibemagazine.com)
- History of the Smash, June 12, 2013

Internet Movie Database: (www.imdb.com)
- **Treehouse of Horror/The Simpsons**, Episode aired Oct 25, 1990
- **Sandy's Rocket/Squeaky Boots**, Episode aired Sep 23, 1999

Library of Congress: (www.loc.gov)
- **"Sgt. Pepper's Lonely Hearts Club Band"—The Beatles (1967)** Added to the National Registry: 2003 Essay by Bob Spitz (guest post)*

Lura's Kitchen - It's All in the Mix: (luraskitchen.com)
- **A Sweet Memory, Teacakes in History**, August 31, 2023, Lura Daniels-Ball

Massachusetts Historical Society-Founded 1791: (www.masshist.org)
- Object of The Month: **The Boston Roots of Edgar Allan Poe**, *January 2009*

Munchery - eat better at home: (www.munchery.com)
- **Chowder: an Icon of American Cooking**, April 29, 2023

National Geographic - Traveler (UK): (www.nationalgeographic.com)
- The story behind the Philly cheesesteak, Tom Burson, October 10, 2024

National Park Service: (www.nps.gov)
- **The Mystery of Edgar Allan Poe's Death,** Edgar Allan Poe National Historic Site, February 24, 2021
- **Fort Moultrie**, February 5, 2023
- **Edgar Allan Poe**, January 30, 2023

National Public Radio: (www.npr.org)
- **Peach Wars: Southern States Spar Over Which Has The Most Juice**, Clare Lombardo, July 6, 2018

Old Line Plate: (oldlineplate.com)
- **Crab Cakes**, (True History of), September 28, 2017

P to W

Phrase Finder: (www.phrases.org.uk)
- *Revenge is a Dish Best Served Cold Origin, Gary Martin, 1997-2024*

Poe Baltimore: (www.poeinbaltimore.org)
- *Poe History in Baltimore, Edgar Allan Poe Society in Baltimore, 2025*

Poe Museum - Richmond, Virginia: (**www.poemuseum.org**)

Poe's Tavern: (**www.poestavern.com**)
- Sullivan's Island, South Carolina

Pop Poetry: (**poppoetry.substack.com**)
- **The Reluctant Witchy Icon Who Adapted a Poe Classic,** Revisiting Stevie Nicks' "Annabel Lee," just in time for Scorpio season. Caitlin Cowan, Nov 02, 2022.

Scalar - USC: (**scalar.usc.edu**)
- **Edgar Allan Poe : Portrayal in the Media: an Annotated Bibliography of Edgar Allan Poe as a character**, Vanessa Rodriguez, *Batman: Nevermore*, Graphic Novel (1/4)

Sagamore Rye: (**sagamorespirit.com**)
- **Cocktails Crafted for Sharing**, 2025

Sipsmith - London: (**sipsmith.com**)
- **How London Dry Gin Came to Be—And Why We Made It Our Own** in Gin Culture, **May 24, 2018**

Tiki Forum: (**tikiforum.com**)
- **Missionary's Downfall**, September 10, 2021

What's Cooking America: (**whatscookingamerica.net**)
- **Boston Cream Pie History and Recipe**

ABOUT THE AUTHORS 6

THE

AUTHORS

CARMEN BOULDIN

Carmen Bouldin works as an English teacher. She has worked in education since 2004. In her spare time, she writes gothic romance, mystery, and poetry. Much of her writing and art is inspired by Edgar Allan Poe. She recently published her first novella, *The Rose Bush*. Three of her more romantic poems were published in Ravens Quoth Press' romantic poetry anthology, *Cherish 2*. Her poem, "The Raven's Mourning," was published in the anthology, *Evermore 4*, by Ravens Quoth Press in 2024 and was nominated for a Saturday Visiter Award in 2020. She also cohosts a podcast, The Six Degrees of Edgar A. Poe, where she and her POEcast partner, Jeanie Smith, discuss Poe's influences on multiple genres. She also enjoys creating visual art. Her painting, "There's no Place like Poe," was nominated for a Saturday Visiter Award in 2019. A native Memphian, Carmen, resides in Middle Tennessee with her husband, Jeff, and their two cats, tuxedo cat-Mitt and solid black cat-Poe. Carmen and Jeff love to travel and wear vintage inspired attire Carmen creates through the art of sewing.

JEFF BOULDIN

Jeff has worked in the security industry for around thirty years. When he was younger, he took on a second job as a bartender for around six years, where he learned about mixing cocktails, especially balancing flavors. His expertise has been a huge asset in developing the cocktails in this book.

In his spare time, Jeff is a Bourbon aficionado and enjoys smoking cigars. He is an avid reader, he enjoys a variety of music, and he enjoys hiking and backpacking. He has three grown daughters, and his middle daughter just made him a grandpa. Jeff enjoys travelling with Carmen, creating new adventures wherever they trek.

JEANIE SMITH

I am a retired veteran teacher of 18 years in the subjects of math, science, history, theatre arts, and language arts, to name a few. As you could probably guess, I loved being a renaissance woman. Reading, writing, creating, no matter what the art, was meant to be expressed not hidden away like a skeleton secret too ashamed to share. Which has brought me back into a world of Edgar Allan Poe and my love of education.

Along with my POEtastic partner, Carmen Bouldin, I get to once again impart my many loves from creating to educating onto a brand new audience in a purview suited to grow for many years into the POEmorrow!

LEVI LIONEL LELAND

Levi is an independent Edgar Allan Poe scholar from Rhode Island. He has specialized on Poe's ties to Providence and on Sarah Helen Whitman (the poetess from Providence to whom Poe was engaged for a brief time in 1848). Levi created and guides "A Walking Tour of Poe's Providence" that had a successful debut in 2021. To learn more about Edgar Allan Poe and Sarah Helen Whitman in Providence, visit Levi's website at edgarallanpoeri.com. You can also find him on Facebook and Instagram by searching "Levi Lionel Leland." Please check out his 2025 Simon and Schuster release titled **Edgar Allan Poe**, *The Master of the Macabre.*

HOW TO FIND US

The Six Degrees of Edgar Allan Poe

Website: www.sixdegreesofpoe.com

Facebook: The 6 Degrees of Edgar Allan Poe

Instagram: @sixdegreesofpoe

X: @sixdegreesofpoe

YouTube: https://www.youtube.com/@poeunplugged3978

Patreon: patreon.com/SixDegreesofEdgarAllanPoe

Levi Leland

Website: https://edgarallanpoeri.com/

Facebook: https://www.facebook.com/llleland

facebook.com/groups/friendsofsarahhelenwhitman

Instagram: https://www.instagram.com/levi_lionel_leland/